# THE
# POWER ELITE
## THEIR HISTORY & FUTURE

Unless otherwise specified, all Scriptures are taken from the King James Version of the Holy Bible.

**The Power Elite: Their History and Future**
© 2012, Dennis L. Cuddy

All rights reserved under International Copyright Law. No part of this book may be used or reproduced in any manner whatsoever without written permission of the publisher, except in the case of brief quotations in articles and reviews. For more information write: Bible Belt Publishing, 500 Beacon Dr., Oklahoma City, OK 73127, (800) 652-1144, *www.swrc.com*.

*Printed in the United States of America*

ISBN 1-933641-50-9

# THE
# POWER ELITE
## THEIR HISTORY & FUTURE

DENNIS L. CUDDY, Ph.D.

# Table of Contents

Introduction .................................................... 7

The Knights Templar ............................................ 9

The Power Elite's Historical Outline ............................ 14

The Illuminati ................................................. 28

The Psychological Conditioning of Americans ................... 55

The Power Elite's Use of Misdirection .......................... 61

Oklahoma City Bombing Anniversary ........................... 68

A "Bold New World" and "Forces Too Powerful" ................. 76

The Power Elite and the Muslim Brotherhood ................... 106

Looming Economic Disaster .................................... 125

The Election of 2012 . . . and the Future ....................... 130

Looking Backward ............................................. 136

Index .......................................................... 159

About the Author .............................................. 176

In Benjamin Disraeli's *Coningsby: or the New Generation* (1844), the key character is Sidonia, who says: "So you see, my dear Coningsby, that the world is governed by very different personages from what is imagined by those who are not behind the scenes."

# Introduction

The cartoon opposite this page is from the *St. Louis Post-Dispatch* in 1911, and shows Power Elite (PE) members John D. Rockefeller, J. P. Morgan, and others welcoming Karl Marx to Wall Street. Under Marx's arm is a book, but it is not his *Communist Manifesto*. Rather, the book is titled *Socialism*, because the ultimate goal of the PE is a synthesis of Western capitalism and Eastern communism into a world socialist government (WSG).

The history of the PE goes back at least to the time of the Knights Templar almost a thousand years ago, and therefore this book begins with them. Because of the tremendous wealth the Templars amassed over hundreds of years, kings and queens were even beholden to them.

A useful starting point, though, for the historical outline of the "modern" PE would be about three hundred and fifty years ago. And this part of the book covers their political and economic activities, followed by their alteration of nations' values to accept the PE's control.

A critical moment in the PE's plan for global dominance occurred almost 250 years ago with the founding of the Illuminati in 1776. Not only did the Illuminati advocate the overthrow of monarchical authority, but religious authority (biblical values) as well. This book covers the methods the PE has used to bring this about, including psychological conditioning and misdirection.

Looking at our recent times, the book next presents the Oklahoma City bombing as an example of misdirection. This is followed by an extensive look at how a "bold new world" is being shaped by the PE using coercive means to undermine national sovereignty and bring about a world socialist government (WSG).

Currently the Middle East and North Africa are the focus of international attention, and the book analyzes the role of the Muslim Brotherhood (MB) in the PE's plan. And the driving mechanism to bring about the plan's fulfillment is economics, so the book next reveals the looming economic disaster created by the PE to further its goals.

This is followed by a look at the election of 2012, and the importance of President Obama's reelection for the PE as he moves the United States closer toward socialism. Finally, the book contains a section titled "Looking Backward," which, like Edward Bellamy's classic work of 1887, projects into the future to see how the PE's ultimate plan for a world socialist government was fulfilled.

Just as my book *New World Order: The Rise of Techno-Feudalism* was largely a collection of my NewsWithViews.com columns, so also is this one.

# The Knights Templar

The film series *National Treasure* begins with a young Ben Gates' grandfather telling him about a secret treasure found by the Knights Templar about a thousand years ago. He said it was brought to America by Freemasons who "left us clues [on the back of the dollar bill] like these: the unfinished pyramid, the all-seeing eye, symbols of the Knights Templar, guardians of the treasure. They're speaking to us through these" regarding the location of the treasure here.

In the eleventh century A.D., Hasan-i Sabbah became the founder and first grand master of the Assassins. According the a famous Ismaili story, he had gone to school with Omar Khayyam, who wrote:

> Dear Love, Couldst thou and I with fate conspire
> To grasp this sorry scheme of things entire.
> Would we not shatter it to bits, and then
> Remould it nearer to the heart's desire!

The last line of this later became the motto of the Fabian socialists, as in their famous stained-glass window two of their leaders are seen about to shatter the world to bits upon an anvil.

In 1118, the Burgundian knight Hugues de Payens founded and became first grand master of the Order of the Temple (of Solomon), also referred to as the Knights Templar. They were modeled after the Assassins' attire in that the knights wore red crosses on a white background similar in color to Assassins' rafiqs, and they wore red caps and belts and white tunics.

Prior to the Templars, the Order of Sion had been founded in 1090 just south of Jerusalem by Godfroi de Bouillon, and in R. Rohricht's *Regesta Regni Hierosolymitani* (1893), there is a charter dated May 2, 1125, with the name of Prior Arnaldus at Sion linked to Hugues de Payens. After a later Templar grand master, Gerard de Ridefort, lost Jerusalem to the Saracens in 1187, the Order of Sion separated from the Templars.

This was the time of the Crusades, during which Richard the Lion-Hearted fled from the Holy Land disguised as a Templar. The Templars by the early 1300s had amassed great wealth, and English king after king was in constant debt to them. King Philip IV of France plotted to take their wealth by accusing them of plotting against the thrones of Europe as well as against the church, and he had their grand master, Jacques de Molay, and three others burned at the stake in Paris on March 18, 1313. De Molay denied he had been guilty of spitting on the cross and of denying Christ, but the *Encyclopedia of Occultism and Parapsychology* says that the Templars had introduced gnosticism into their rites, and had "institutionalized homosexuality in their Order."

We are generally told that with the execution of de Molay, the Templars organizationally ceased to exist as an entity. However, in the 1874 edition of C. G. Addison's *The Knights Templars* (originally published in 1842), on page 541 there is a list of the grand masters of the Templars from de Molay (1313) to Sir William Sidney Smith (1838). The list comes from Albert Mackey's *Lexicon of Freemasonry* published in 1855.

There is some controversy over whether the list is legitimate, but it seems clear that de Molay, anticipating his own death, appointed John Mark Larmenius his successor as grand master. In Addison's book, it states:

> The Charter by which the supreme authority has been transmitted [from de Molay to Larmenius] is judicial and conclusive evidence

of the Order's continued existence. This Charter of transmission, with the signatures of the various Chiefs of the Temple, is preserved at Paris, with the ancient statutes of the Order, the rituals, the records, the seals, the standards, and other memorials of the early Templars. . . . The Grand Master Bernard Raymond, in 1838, was succeeded in the regency of the Order by Admiral William Sidney Smith, who held sway till his death in 1840; and that at that date it numbered amongst the British subjects enrolled as its office-bearers the names of the Duke of Sussex, Grand Prior of England; the Duke of Leinster, Grand Prior of Ireland; the Earl of Durham, Grand Prior of Scotland; the Chevalier Burnes (Grand Master of Scottish Freemasons in India), Grand Preceptor of Southern Asia; the Chevalier Tennyson D'Eyncourt, Grand Prior of Italy; General George Wright, Grand Prior of India, etc. etc. . . .

We know that all of the Knights Templar were not captured or killed by King Philip IV in France at the time their leader, Jacques de Molay, was burned at the stake, because some of their graves have been found in Kilmartin, Scotland, dating back to the early fourteenth century. Masonic leader Albert Pike has indicated that before de Molay died, he instituted what came to be known as the occult Hermetic or Scottish Masonry, the lodges of which were later established in Naples, Edinburgh, Stockholm, and Paris. In this latter city, the lodge was the Grand Orient, perhaps one of the most occultic.

Sir William Sidney Smith was a former admiral of the British navy who had supposedly been given a Templar cross (left by Richard the Lion-Hearted) by a Greek archbishop. Associated with Smith at this time was Chevalier (Charles) Tennyson D'Eyncourt mentioned above. He was the uncle of Alfred Lord Tennyson, who wrote in "Locksley Hall" (1842) about "the Parliament of man, the Federation of the world." The latter Tennyson was also a member of the Society for Psychical Research, about which I have written previously elsewhere. What is notable about the former Tennyson being Grand Prior of Italy, General Wright being Grand Prior of India, etc., is that the work of these new Templars of the nineteenth century was global!

What may have happened was that from the beginning of the fourteenth century to the middle of the sixteenth century, the Templars perhaps merged with the Hospitallers, as there are references to the "Order of the Knights of St. John and the Temple." In J. Maidment's *Templaria* (1828–1830), there is a charter granted by King James IV of Scotland dated 1488 which refers to "Fratribus Hospitalis Hierosolymitani, Militibus Templi Solomonis" and seems to indicate recognition of the continued existence of the Templars in some form.

On the cover of the 1987 edition of *Knight Templar* is a picture of "Jonathan Swift, Satirist." Swift was probably the illegitimate son of Sir William Temple, to whom I will refer in my next chapter, "The Power Elite's Historical Outline." Swift was descended from the Templars because Sir William Temple's family was descended from a Knight Templar in Leicester, England, in the 1100s. And one of Swift's friends was Alexander Pope, who wrote:

> Vice is a monster of so frightful mien
> As to be hated, needs but to be seen;
> Yet seen too oft, familiar with her face,
> We first endure, then pity, then embrace."

Relevant to this Pope epigram is the following from the 1874 edition of Addison's *The Knights Templars*. It is from an account of the fall of Jerusalem to the Muslim leader Saladin during the Crusades in which the Templars were involved in October 1187, and reads as follows:

> Barefoot processions of women, monks, and priests were continually made to the Holy Sepulcher to implore the Son of God to save his tomb and his inheritance from impious violation. The females, as a mark of humility and distress, cut off their hair and cast it to the winds. The ladies of Jerusalem made their daughters do penance

by standing up to their necks in tubs of cold water placed upon Calvary. But it availed nought, for our Lord Jesus Christ, says the chronicler, would not listen to any prayer that they made. For the filth, the luxury, and the adultery which prevailed in the city did not suffer prayer or supplication to ascend before God.

Could this be what awaits America and its people and for the same reasons?

# The Power Elite's Historical Outline

The Power Elite (PE) has been around for centuries, but a useful starting point for its "modern activities" would be about three hundred and fifty years ago. In 1677, Sir William Temple (a sort of John J. McCloy PE agent) helped arrange the marriage of William of Orange (Holland) to Princess Mary (heir to the British throne). In 1688, another PE agent, Thomas Wharton, instigated the Revolution of 1688 replacing James II (a Stuart) with William and Mary as rulers of Britain. Shortly thereafter, William had the British treasury borrow heavily from the Bank of Amsterdam, whose bankers received a royal charter to establish the Bank of England which, by 1698, was owed 16 million pounds by the British treasury. Indebtedness of sovereigns and nations is one of the primary means of PE control.

Wharton was a Hanoverian, as was George III, who became king of England in 1760. Shortly thereafter, the American colonies began to print their own script for currency, and the PE resented this movement of economic independence. Therefore, the British crown began to enact measures (e.g., Stamp Act) to counter this, and according to founding father Benjamin Franklin, this was largely the cause of the Declaration of Independence on July 4, 1776. This revolution of independence led to the establishment of the U.S., resulting in a plan by the PE to regain control of America. How the PE would do this was explained by Philip Freneau in the July 1792 edition of *American*

*Museum.* And the process the PE would use is the dialectic, and they created communism as the antithesis to American capitalism.

In 1828, the first commune in the U.S. was founded in New Harmony, Indiana, by Robert Dale Owen and Frances Wright. Shortly thereafter, in New York they formed the Workingmen's Party with Orestes Brownson who would later describe their plot to take control of the U.S. (See my two hundred-year *Chronology of Education with Quotable Quotes.*) The PE-controlled League of the Just financed Karl Marx to write the *Communist Manifesto* in 1848, and Marx's slogan would be "Workers of the World, Unite."

In an effort to break up the U.S., the PE fomented the American Civil War. In 1861, U.S. minister to Vienna John Lothrop Motley wrote about a plot to break the Southern states from the others, forming with Caribbean and Central American nations a "Gulf Empire." Motley said the plot began about twenty-five years earlier, which would be about the time of the attempted assassination of President Andrew Jackson on January 30, 1835, by Richard Lawrence. When Lawrence was asked about his motive, he replied that "money would be more plenty" and would be more easily obtained from the Second Bank of the United States which Jackson opposed.

When asked if anyone advised him to shoot President Jackson, Lawrence replied, "I do not like to say," and he further declared that no power in this country could punish him for having attempted to assassinate President Jackson "because it would be resisted by the powers of Europe, as well as of this country." Lawrence also said he had been "long in correspondence with the powers of Europe" (see report written by Dr. Causin and Dr. Thomas Sewell of Washington, D.C., after interviewing Richard Lawrence).

The PE in Europe owned a sizable portion of the Second Bank of the United States, and in Europe in the early 1840s Alfred Lord Tennyson in "Locksley Hall" wished for "the Parliament of man, the Federation of the world." As far as John Ruskin was concerned, this world government would be run by "the best northern blood" elite.

Ruskin matriculated at Oxford University in 1836, only a few years after the secret Skull & Bones (S&B) elite society was founded at Yale University. The elitist Ruskin has a swastika on his gravestone, and swastikas (elitist symbol) have been in the S&B vault at Yale. In 1869, Ruskin began teaching at Oxford, and in the 1870s Oxford student Cecil Rhodes was impressed by Ruskin's philosophy to such an extent that in 1891 Rhodes formed the Secret Society of the Elect "to take the government of the whole world" in Rhodes' own words.

By the early 1900s, hereditary PE member John D. Rockefeller had his agents in every hamlet in the land (see Thomas Lawson's *Frenzied Finance,* 1904) and a 1911 *St. Louis Post-Dispatch* cartoon by Robert Minor shows Rockefeller with fellow PE members J. P. Morgan, Andrew Carnegie, etc. welcoming Karl Marx's "socialism" to Wall Street. Also in 1911, PE agent Col. Edward M. House's *Philip Dru: Administrator* was published and referred to a socialist future to come, "socialism as dreamed of by Karl Marx." House was President Woodrow Wilson's chief advisor, and Wilson was aware of "a power somewhere so organized, so subtle, so watchful, so interlocked, so complete, so pervasive...."

One of the top members of Cecil Rhodes' secret society was Lord Esher who helped involve the U.S. in WWI, which Colonel House said had to be "in fierce and exaggerated form" to bring about Tennyson's desire in the form of the League of Nations. The American people, though, rejected the League, so the next phase of the PE's dialectical synthesis of thesis (capitalism) and antithesis (communism) resulting in socialism was the creation of National Socialism (which is what "NAZI" means).

Colonel House had succeeded in getting President Wilson to sign the Federal Reserve Act in 1913. The "Fed" was under the control of PE members like J. P. Morgan, who would then establish the Bank for International Settlements (BIS) in 1930. In November 1933, President Franklin Roosevelt wrote to Colonel House that they both knew the U.S. government was under the control of "a financial element in our larger centers" ever since the days of President Jackson. The BIS was the central bank of all the world's central banks, and beginning in the 1930s it came under the control of the Nazis with American Thomas McKittrick heading the BIS from 1940 to 1946.

In 1933, in *The Shape of Things to Come*, PE agent H. G. Wells wrote that a second world war would begin around 1939, and in that year his new world order indicated Tennyson's world-state would come from a conference in Basra, Iraq, in about five decades. The reason Wells said this was that he knew the second attempt (the U.N. at the end of WWII) to bring about Tennyson's dream also wouldn't succeed.

Because the PE's plan involved using National Socialism (Nazism) to bring about the synthesis of capitalism and communism into a world socialist government, the brains of the Nazi movement (Himmler, Bormann, etc.) developed a secret plan to control much of the world's economy within two generations (about now), and with a continued alliance with the Muslim Brotherhood beginning in the 1930s until today.

Regarding the Power Elite's (PE's) plan for a world socialist government brought about by a dialectical synthesis of Western capitalism and Eastern communism, Ford Foundation president H. Rowan Gaither told congressional Reece Committee research director Norman Dodd that they were under directives from the White House to so alter American life as to bring about a "comfortable merger" of the U.S. with the Soviet Union. Similarly, in 1962 when CFR member Lincoln Bloomfield wrote a report for secretary of state Dean Rusk (Rhodes scholar) indicating that "if the communist dynamic was greatly abated, the West might lose whatever incentive it has for world government."

The "communist dynamic" expressed itself at this time in the Vietnam War, involving the West against the Soviet and Chinese communists (brought to power in 1949 by PE agent Gen. George Marshall) via their proxies, the North Vietnamese and Vietcong. This was another "no-win war" (like the Korean War) that reduced the support for nationalistic patriotism among young American adults (and, as in most wars, killed off many of the strongest young patriotic men). This was a necessary part of the PE's plan if there was to be a transference of loyalties from the nation-state to a larger world socialist government.

A transference directly from the nation-state to a stage before the world government would be to regional associations. In the October 1967 edition of the CFR's *Foreign Affairs*, Richard Nixon wrote of regional arrangements that would evolve into a "new world order." This same theme would be picked up by Zbigniew Brzezinski (ZB) at Mikhail Gorbachev's first State of the World Forum in 1995 where ZB declared: "We cannot leap into world government through one quick step. . . . The precondition for eventual and genuine globalization is progressive regionalization because by that we move toward larger, more stable, more cooperative units."

ZB in 1973 became the first director of the Trilateral Commission, established by PE member David Rockefeller, who worked with various communist dictators over the years. This also fit within the PE's dialectical process, for while David Rockefeller worked with the communists, his brother, Nelson, had worked with the Nazis.

After Ronald Reagan was elected president in 1980, the dialectical movement toward a "comfortable merger" of the U.S. and U.S.S.R. continued, as Reagan decreasingly referred to the Soviet Union as an "evil empire," instead implementing in 1986 the Soviet-American Exchange Agreement with Gorbachev after the latter became general-secretary of the Soviet Union in March 1985.

George H. W. Bush succeeded Reagan as president, and in 1990 emphasized the need for a "new world order." Gorbachev followed this with his May 6, 1992, speech in Fulton, Missouri, in which he said the following (some of which was *not* printed in the American press): "This is not just some ordinary stage of development like many others in world history. . . . An awareness of the need of some kind of global government is gaining ground. . . . A powerful process of technical and political internationalization is taking place. . . ."

At the end of 1992, Bill Clinton was elected president, and (as a Rhodes scholar) he supported a world government which was longed for by Cecil Rhodes. In keeping with the regionalism-first strategy of the PE, NAFTA was begun in January 1994, just two months after the European Union (EU) in November 1993.

The current economic crisis in the EU is to coerce its members to take the next step in the PE's plan, which would be fiscal union in a United States of Europe. At his address to the Masonic Peace Conference in Paris in 1849, Victor Hugo had said, "Let us have a United States of Europe; let us have a continental federation." In Lenin's *Collected Works* (Vol. 21), he called for a United States of Europe (including Russia), as did Stalin in 1926. Winston Churchill had an essay titled "The United States of Europe" published in *The Saturday Evening Post* on February 15, 1930, and he echoed this call in October 1942 to his cabinet and in Zurich in 1946.

Moving this theme forward, German chancellor Angela Merkel on June 4, 2012, pronounced, "We need more Europe, not less." And in "Europe's foreign ministers want more power for EU" (*Welt Online*, June 21, 2012), one finds that among the interim recommendations of the "Future Group" on the EU are that there should be a single, directly elected EU president, the creation of an EU army, European rather than national visas, and more direct control of national budgets.

George W. Bush in 2000 was elected president following Bill Clinton's two terms, and Bush's secretary of education, Rod Paige, on October 3, 2003, declared that the U.S. was pleased to rejoin UNESCO where we could develop common strategies to prepare our children to become "citizens of the world," a title which Barack Obama (elected president in 2008) would use to identify himself.

It was then the beginning of the twenty-first century, which Aldous Huxley in *Brave New World Revisited* (1958) said would be "the era of World Controllers." Confirming this was PE member

David Rockefeller's startling admission in his *Memoirs* (2002) that he was part of a "secret cabal" which was "conspiring with others around the world to build a more integrated political and economic structure—one world, if you will." That the cabal is "secret" means its members are not all known. At the beginning of the Prologue in Nicholas Hagger's *The Syndicate: The Story of the Coming World Government* (2004), he reveals that the Queen of England is alleged to have told her butler, Paul Burrell, a few months after Princess Diana's death in a car crash (August 31, 1997): "Be careful. There are powers at work in this country about which we have no knowledge."

In following the PE's strategy of using a dialectical process via regionalization to achieve a world socialist government, Barack Obama was elected president in 2008. With his Muslim background, he would be able to relate to the Muslim revolutionary uprisings in North Africa and the Middle East beginning in 2011. He made presidential overtures to the Muslim Brotherhood (MB) from the beginning of his administration. And as the MB was the leading organizational structure in these revolutions, they would be in a unique cross-countries' position to facilitate the regionalization of the nations involved.

Obama as president could also move the U.S. increasingly toward socialism, which would be necessary for an eventual "comfortable merger" with other socialist regions such as Europe and Latin America. He was re-elected (with an "October Surprise") in November 2012. He could be followed as president by Jeb Bush in 2016 in time to accept the "phoenix" as the new world currency planned for 2018. And if Jeb Bush is re-elected in 2020, the next new president would begin term of office in 2025, the year by which Luciferian occultist Alice Bailey proclaimed the "World Federation of Nations" would be "taking rapid shape," according to "the Plan."

In the first part of this chapter, I outlined the political and economic aspects of the Power Elite's (PE's) activities over hundreds of years using the dialectical process. The PE could not achieve ultimate success, however, unless they could shift the values of the people away from those of *The Holy Bible* toward those of the secular humanists today.

On May 1, 1776, Adam Weishaupt founded the Illuminati not only to overthrow monarchical authority, but also religious authority, promoting the concept of "Do what thou wilt." Dispersing in the 1780s, the Illuminati in France infiltrated Masonic lodges and helped to foment the French Revolution which began in 1789. The revolutionists not only overthrew the Bourbons (ruling family of France from 1589 to 1793), but also sought to destroy the religious authority of the Catholic Church, symbolically placing a prostitute on the altar at Notre Dame Cathedral. During this period of revolution against religious values, the Marquis de Sade (from whom comes the word "sadist") advocated abortion as a necessary means of population control in his *La Philosophie Dans le Boudoir* in 1795.

In the early 1800s, the Marquis de Lafayette brought Madame Francoise d'Arusmont to the United States. Going by the name Fanny Wright, in 1828 she joined Robert Owen at his first commune in America, established in New Harmony, Indiana, in 1825. Owen said, "I am come to this country [U.S.A.] to introduce an entire new order of society." And Wright was an apostle of free marital union, birth control, etc.

In 1829, Wright and Owen's son, Robert Dale Owen, joined with Orestes Brownson to form the Workingmen's Party, with Brownson later revealing: "The great object was to get rid of Christianity, and to convert our churches into halls of science. The plan was to establish a system of state—we said NATIONAL—schools, from which all religion was to be excluded. . . . We were to have godless schools for all the children of the country. . . . The plan has been successfully pursued. . . ."

Apparently sensing what was occurring, Alexis de Tocqueville in 1840 in *Democracy In America* described a potential despotism here by saying: "I do not expect their [democracies'] leaders to be tyrants, but rather schoolmasters." And under such despotism, he indicated that "the will of man is not shattered, but softened, bent, and guided. It does not tyrannize, but it compresses, enervates, extinguishes, and stupefies a people...."

After de Tocqueville's warning appeared, Karl Marx in his economic and philosophic manuscripts of 1844 professed that "Communism begins from the outset with atheism.... Communism, as fully developed naturalism, equals humanism." Four years later, his *Communist Manifesto* was published in 1848. During this same period, French revolutionist the Comte de Saint-Simon's secretary, Auguste Comte, was developing his morally relativistic "Religion of Humanity," and in the 1850s published four volumes describing this *System of Positive Polity*. Relevant to this, on December 8, 1861, Lord Acton wrote to Richard Simpson characterizing a cunning and treacherous group of people, saying "they saw 'no divine part of Christianity,' but divinified humanity, or humanized religion." From Comte's system would come the morally relativistic positivist philosophy, which was adopted by many in the legal profession, ultimately resulting in some federal judges saying the Constitution means whatever they say it means regardless of the founders' original intent.

Then in 1859 and 1871, Charles Darwin wrote his works on evolution, which gave rise to social Darwinism and the alteration of values that went with it. After all, if man were simply an evolved animal with some superior to others, then eugenics would be justified. Picking up on this concept, Prof. John Ruskin at Oxford University believed he and the rest of the Anglo-Saxon elite represented "the best northern blood." This attitude was acted upon by Ruskin disciple Cecil Rhodes, who in 1891 formed the Secret Society of the Elect "to take the government of the whole world," in Rhodes' own words.

Those with "the best northern blood" would be like the "philosopher kings" of Plato's *Republic* and the French Revolution, and considered themselves born to rule the masses. Among the elite were the Rockefellers, who in the early 1900s introduced Margaret Sanger (founder of Planned Parenthood) to those who would support her eugenic causes (e.g., Sanger's *Birth Control Review* for November 1921 said "Birth Control: to create a race of thoroughbreds"), such as reducing the numbers of "dysgenic stock" (inferior humans) among the population.

Material in Sanger's *Pivot of Civilization* (1922) sounds very much like the Nazis' Joseph Goebbels' eugenic declaration about National Socialists (Nazis) in 1938. In *Pivot of Civilization*, Sanger proclaimed that "the most urgent problem today is how to limit and discourage the over-fertility of the mentally and physically defective. Possibly drastic and Spartan methods may be forced upon American society if it continues complacently to encourage the chance and chaotic breeding that has resulted from our stupid, cruel sentimentalism." And Goebbels declared: "Our starting point is not the individual, and we do not subscribe to the view that one should feed the hungry, give drink to the thirsty, or clothe the naked. . . . Our objectives are entirely different: We must have a healthy people in order to prevail in the world."

Combining the model of Owen, Wright, and Brownson (using education to change the values of a people) with Marx's humanism, in 1930 Charles Francis Potter wrote *Humanism: A New Religion*, in which he stated: "Education is thus a most powerful ally of humanism. What can the theistic Sunday schools, meeting for an hour once a week, and teaching only a fraction of the children, do to stem the tide of a five-day program of humanistic teaching?" Three years later, the "Father of Progressive Education," John Dewey, along with Potter and others, co-authored the atheistic *Humanist Manifesto* in 1933.

Continuing the tactic of using education to alter the religious values of society, John R. Rees of the Tavistock Institute for Medical Psychology delivered a speech on June 18, 1940 (*Mental Health*, October 1940), in which he explained regarding mental health professionals: "Public life, politics, and industry should all of them be within our sphere of influence. . . . We have made a useful attack upon a number of professions. The two easiest of them naturally are the teaching profession and the church. . . . ." To the PE, perhaps the major obstacle to the implementation of their plan was the concept of moral absolutes (right vs. wrong) as taught by the church. Furthering the "attack" (Rees' term) upon these values via education, Brock Chisholm (head of the World Health Organization and close friend of communist spy Alger Hiss) published an article in the February 1946 edition of *Psychiatry*, in which he revealed their strategy that "a program of re-education or a new kind of education" needed to be charted to "help our children to carry out their responsibilities as world citizens. . . . We have swallowed all manner of poisonous certainties fed us by our parents, our Sunday and day school teachers, our politicians, our priests. . . . The reinterpretation and eventual eradication of the concept of right and wrong, . . . the substitution of intelligent and rational thinking for faith in the certainties of old people, these are the belated objectives . . . for charting the changes in human behavior."

Secular humanist leader John Dewey's greatest influence was through Columbia University's Teachers College. By the mid-1950s, this college was producing about one-third of the presidents and deans at accredited teacher training institutions, about twenty percent of all public school teachers, and over one-fourth of the superintendents of schools in the largest 168 cities in the U.S. By the early 1960s, Dewey's "progressive" education was in almost every school in the land.

The next step for the PE, of course, was to rid these schools (as Orestes Brownson said) of the influence of *The Holy Bible* and prayer. This came with the Supreme Court's banning of Bible reading and school prayer in *Engel v. Vital* (1962) and *Abington v. Schempp* (1963).

With these two underpinnings of American society banned, the values still taught in the public schools were determined by the morally autonomous decision-making of individual students, which is an important characteristic of Dewey's secular humanism. Expressing this philosophy was education leader Ted Sizer in his (co-authored with his wife, Nancy) Introduction to *Five Lectures . . . On Moral*

*Education* (1970), in which he declared: "Christian sermonizing denies individual autonomy. . . . No longer can we list . . . objective 'truths' about the world and expect children to take them over intact. . . . Clearly the strict adherence to a 'code' is out of date." This was critically important to the success of the PE's plan because, as President Abraham Lincoln explained, "The philosophy of the classroom in one generation will be the philosophy of government in the next."

Three years later, the second atheistic *Humanist Manifesto* was published, and the Supreme Court handed down the baby-killing *Roe v. Wade* decision allowing abortions. The decision could easily have been undone by Congress simply limiting the federal courts' jurisdiction in this matter, but this has not been done even by today, which shows how the once-biblical morality of the people has been severely weakened.

The attack upon our traditional values has covered many aspects of our lives. In the November 14, 1981, edition of *The Nation,* feminist activist Ellen Willis wrote that "feminism is . . . the cutting edge of a revolution in cultural and moral values. . . . The objective of every feminist reform, from legal abortion to the ERA to child-care programs, is to undermine traditional family values. . . ."

In the 1980s, elementary school children in several large school systems were taught the theme from the TV show "M*A*S*H," which is "Suicide Is Painless," with lyrics proclaiming that "cheating is the only way to win, the game of life is lost anyway, and suicide is painless." And in 1987, two federal appeals court rulings continued to undermine biblical values. On August 24 of that year, an appeals court overturned Judge Brevard Hand's decision that the religion of secular humanism was being taught via certain Alabama textbooks, for example, teaching students they should make their own decisions about whether to shoplift or illegally buy drugs. And two days later, another appeals court overturned Judge Thomas Hull's ruling, and said Tennessee students could be required to read prayers to idols and be taught that Jesus was an illiterate.

By 1990, a Girl Scouts survey found that sixty-five percent of high school students would cheat on an important exam. On January 22 of the same year, on NBC's "Today Show," Dr. Michael Lewis of the New Jersey Robert Wood Johnson Medical School said, "Lying is an important part of social life, and children who are unable to do it are children who may have developmental problems." The "Today Show" host didn't challenge this outrageous claim!

The next year, James Patterson's and Peter Kim's *The Day America Told the Truth—What People Really Believe About Everything That Really Matters* was published and detailed poll results showing Americans are "making up their own moral codes" (this is what Sizer said would happen). The polls further showed nine of ten citizens reported that they lie regularly, one-third of all married Americans indicating they've had an affair, and seven percent saying that for $10 million dollars they would kill a stranger! Patterson's and Kim's survey also found one in five women saying they had been date-raped, but this shouldn't be surprising given that characters like Luke on "General Hospital," Ross on "All My Children," and John on "As the World Turns" all raped women and became heroes later on these soap operas.

The assault upon biblical values continued through the 1990s and up to today, as the consciousness of the country is being changed. Recently, there have been TV ads for country music songs of the 1970s and 1980s, including Barbara Mandrell singing that if loving a particular man is wrong, she doesn't want to be right; and Kenny Rogers sings a duet saying they don't need tomorrow if they have tonight. The implications of such songs are clear. There are several good songs, like Marty Robbins singing "My Woman, My Woman, My Wife." But those are greatly outnumbered by songs such as "Heaven's Just a Sin Away." If the airwaves have pounded people's minds for decades with messages like these, should the moral degeneration that has occurred be surprising to anyone?

Americans have also accepted presidents who have lied to them and who have not stopped the massive killings by abortion. To the extent that Americans have rejected the Word of God in these matters, they have instead followed Adam Weishaupt's (and Lucifer's) immoral teaching "Do what thou wilt." Relevant to this, Luciferian Alice Bailey said in 1933 that according to "The Plan," the World Federation of Nations would be "taking rapid shape" by 2025. And this will result in the fulfillment of the PE's ultimate goal of a secular humanist world socialist government not too long afterward.

# The Illuminati

The Illuminati (called "The Order" by its members) was a secret society founded on May 1, 1776, by Adam Weishaupt. According to University of Edinburgh professor (and general-secretary of the Royal Society of Edinburgh) John Robison in *Proofs of a Conspiracy* (1798), its purpose was to root out all religion and ordinary morality, abolish national distinctions, demean patriotism, and "rule the world."

Weishaupt had been a Jesuit and professor of canon law at the University at Ingolstadt (Bavaria), and he initially called his secret society Perfektibilisten. According to Will and Ariel Durant in *Rousseau and Revolution* (1967), Weishaupt "followed the model of the Society of Jesus [Jesuits], divided his associates into grades of initiation, and pledged them to obey their leaders in a campaign to 'unite all men capable of independent thought,' make man 'a masterpiece of reason, and thus attain highest perfection in the art of government.'" Weishaupt said, "Reason will be the only code of man.... When at last reason becomes the religion of man, so will the problem be solved." To Weishaupt (Illuminati code name "Spartacus"), the "problem" was all authority, monarchical and religious, as well as ownership of private property.

Weishaupt believed that he had developed a plan that could not be stopped, saying "my means are effectual, and irresistible. Our secret association works in a way that nothing can withstand." A key component of his plan included directing academic and religious education. If the Illuminati "was to govern the world," as they believed, they had to "acquire the direction of education—of church management—of the professorial chair, and the pulpit" (Robison, page 109). From Illuminati "secret correspondence" Robison found their "Instruction B for the whole degree of Regent" that included winning "the common people in every corner. This will be done chiefly by means of the schools, and by open, hearty behavior, show condescension, popularity and toleration of their prejudices which we shall at leisure root out and dispel."

According to Friedrich Christoph Schlosser's *History of the eighteenth century and of the nineteenth till the overthrow of the French Empire: With particular reference to mental cultivation and progress* (Vol. IV, 1845), the Illuminati was particularly interested in princes, declaring that their "grand object shall be to disseminate true knowledge among classes, and to bring the ruling princes under guardianship of the order." One way the Illuminati did this was to place their members as tutors of the children of nobility, especially princes who would later become rulers of countries. Such is the case of Alexander I of Russia who came under the influence of the Illuminati at a young age.

The secret correspondence of the Illuminati also revealed their plan to use the liberation of women for their purposes, as it stated:

> There is no way of influencing men so powerfully as by means of the women. These should therefore be our chief study; we should insinuate ourselves into their good opinion, give them hints of emancipation from the tyranny of public opinion and of standing up for themselves; it will be an immense relief to their enslaved minds to be freed from any one bond of restraint, and it will fire them more, and cause them to work for us with zeal, without knowing that they do so; for they will only be indulging their own desire of personal admiration.

Concerning religious education, Terry Melanson of the online Illuminati Conspiracy Archive said "Weishaupt and his control turned Jesus into a socialist revolutionary: representing Him as a secret society adept, who came to preach egalitarian virtue." In a letter dated September 19, 1776, Weishaupt refers to "our grand master, Jesus of Nazareth."

In terms of morality, Robison indicated the Illuminati's plan included "destroying the veneration for marriage-vows." And he includes a letter from Illuminist Count Ludwig Savioli (code name "Brutus") stating: "The Order must possess the power of life and death in consequence of our Oath . . . by the same right that any government in the world possesses it: For the Order comes in their place, making them unnecessary." This power of life and death included abortion, as Robison wrote that in the handwriting of Franz Zwack (Weishaupt's closest confidant, and code name "Cato") was "description of a strong box, which, if forced open, shall blow up and destroy its contents—Several receipts for procuring abortion—A composition which blinds or kills when spurted in the face. . . . A method for filling a bed-chamber with pestilential vapours. . . ." Regarding abortion, Weishaupt wrote to confidant Jakob Hertel (code name "Marius") in September 1783 that Weishaupt and his sister-in-law "have tried every method in our power to destroy the child" in her womb.

Not only did the members of the Illuminati have code names, but symbols as well. According to Librarian of Congress and Rhodes scholar James Billington in *Fire in the Minds of Men* (1980), "Weishaupt described his recruitment of Illuminists from within Masonic Lodges in Munich as 'the progress of the [picture of a point in the middle of a circle]' in the political area." Also, if one looks at the Masonic website, one can see the owl as an Illuminati symbol for their Minerval Degree, which was just above the class of Novice. In Greek mythology, Minerva (Pallas-Athene or Athena) was the goddess of wisdom and reason. The Illuminati's Censor at the Minerval Assembly (at night) bows in front of the pyramid painted there. At this point, you might remember the gigantic carved owl present at the Bohemian Grove in California where many of the elite yearly gather in secret.

Robison related that once one became an Illuminatus Minor, "the pupil is warmed by the pictures of universal happiness, and convinced that it is a possible thing to unite all the inhabitants of the earth in one great society. . . . [Then] it may frequently be no hard task to make him think that patriotism is a narrow-minded monopolizing sentiment" (remember President Lyndon Johnson's "Great Society"). In a strategy Fabian socialists later would adopt, the Illuminatus Minor also is told: "We must do our utmost to procure our advancement of Illuminati to all civil offices." Fabian socialist H. G. Wells in *New Worlds for Old* (1907) revealed: "Socialism ceased to be an open revolution, and became a plot. Functions were to be shifted, quietly, unostentatiously, from the representative to the official he appointed: a bureaucracy was to slip into power. . . ."

Baron Adolph von Knigge (code name "Philo") was Weishaupt's second-in-command from 1780 to 1784. And according to Robison, "his favorite scheme" was to create "Citizens of the World." You might reflect at this point whether you have heard any leading political figures recently refer to themselves as "citizens of the world." Thus, whether it's world citizenship, abortion, women's liberation, or some other issue today, one can probably trace its origins back to being part of the Illuminati's plan.

Because world citizenship was an important part of the Illuminati's plot (just as it's an important part of the plan of the Power Elite [PE] today), it is relevant to note that shortly after Ernst von Gochhausen was dismissed from the Illuminati, he wrote a novel titled *Exposure of the Cosmopolitan System: In Letters from ex-Freemasons* (1786), in which the hero asks his superior, "What purpose do the Illuminati have in infiltrating and dominating Masonry?" The response was, "To emancipate all of mankind from religious and political slavery." And the superior continued: "When nations are no longer separated from one another; when citizens are no longer influenced by the exclusive interest of any state or the parochial sentiment of patriotism. . . . World citizenship. What does it mean? You are either a citizen or you are a rebel. There is no third choice...."

Concerning the strategies of the Illuminati, they are similar to those of the PE today. For example, the Illuminati adopted the Machiavellian concept that "the end justifies the means," contrary to the biblical admonition that one should not do evil that "good" may come from it. Today, one can see some of the PE's activities regarding population control as exhibiting the same perspective of "end justifies means."

The plot of the Illuminati began to be exposed by the Bavarian Court of Enquiry which commenced its investigation in 1783, and it concluded with the abolishment of the Illuminati in 1786. There had already been friction within Weishaupt's ranks as Baron Adolph von Knigge (code name "Philo"), who was initiated into the Illuminati in July 1780 and was Weishaupt's second in command, resigned on April 20, 1784, over Weishaupt's direction and dictatorial management of the Order, as revealed in the *Supplement of Further Original Works* (1787) regarding the Illuminati. The next year (1788), Baron von Knigge wrote regarding the Order: "As a rule, under the veil of secrecy, dangerous plans and harmful teachings can be accepted just as well as noble intentions and profound knowledge; because not all members themselves are informed of such depraved intentions, which sometimes tend to lie hidden beneath the beautiful façade. ..." (See Steven Luckert's dissertation titled *Jesuits, Freemasons, Illuminati, and Jacobins: Conspiracy theories, secret societies, and politics in late eighteenth-century Germany.*)

In the same year (1787) the *Supplement of Further Original Works* was published, so was the *Original Writings of the Illuminati* published in Munich by Johann Strobl (code name "Ediles"), who was dismissed by the Order in 1783 and became an ardent opponent of it. Even though the Illuminati had been abolished in 1786, Weishaupt already had a plan for its continuation. In Augustin Barruel's *Memoirs Illustrating the History of Jacobinism* (1798), Weishaupt is quoted as stating: "I have foreseen every thing, and I have prepared every thing.

Let my whole Order go to rack and ruin; in three years I will answer to restore it, and that to a more powerful state than it is in at present. ... I [shall] rise stronger than ever. ... I can sacrifice whole provinces, the desertion of a few individuals, therefore, will not alarm me."

With the abolition of the Illuminati in Bavaria in 1786, Weishaupt fled to the court of Saxe-Gotha under the protection of Duke Ludwig Ernst II, who ruled there and was a high-ranking Illuminatus (code name "Quintus Severus"/"Timoleon"). Ernst II was initiated into the Illuminati in 1783, and today's British royal family are his direct descendants. According to Rene LeForestier in *Les Illumines de Baviere et la Franc-Maconnerie Allemande* (1915), Ernst II on February 25, 1777, had become a member of the Strict Observance Masonic Lodge, and a banquet table was brought in having the shape of a T—"a symbol noticeable on monuments of the old Knights Templar."

Taking over the Illuminati leadership in 1786 was Johann Bode (code name "Aemilius"/"Winefried"), and in 1787 he founded a branch of the Illuminati in the Les Amis Reunis Lodge in Paris. Bode adopted the name Philadelphes, rather than Illuminati, in France. And in an interview with Charles Porset in the December 1995 edition of *Humanisme* (publication of the Grand Orient Masonic Lodge of France), there is reference to a 1789 document holding the Philadelphes responsible for the French Revolution which began that year.

It is entirely logical that the Illuminati would be a prime instigator of the French Revolution, as the theories of French philosopher Jean Jacques Rousseau, who greatly influenced Weishaupt, inspired the Revolution. In addition, according to Librarian of Congress (and Rhodes scholar) James Billington in *Fire in the Minds of Men* (1980): "It was [Jacobin and French revolutionist] Honore Mirabeau's 'evocative' language and his popularization of Illuminist concepts that, during the early years of the Revolution, swayed many of the conspirators in Paris."

Prominent Freemason Marquis de Luchet (who obtained the position of Bibliothèque for Voltaire) in the first year of the Revolution (1789) warned in *Essai Sur La Secte Des Illumines* about the infiltration of the Illuminati into the Masonic lodges, saying:

> You who are misled, or could be, know that there is a conspiracy.... It was formed in the deepest darkness; a society of new beings who know each other without being seen, who understand each other without explanation, who serve without friendship. The goal of the society is world government, taking over the authority of sovereigns, taking their place, and leaving them nothing more than the empty honour of wearing the crown.

The Illuminati not only spread to France, but to other countries as well. According to Le Forestier, King Frederick William II of Prussia wrote to Frederick Augustus I (Elector of Saxony) on October 3, 1789, that he had been informed that "a Masonic sect, who are called Illuminati or Minervals, after having been expelled from Bavaria, have become formidable and have spread rapidly throughout the whole of Germany and into neighboring countries."

In Germany, the philosophical Jacobin Johann Gottlieb Fichte, though not a member of the Illuminati, was accused of having sympathy for them. Fichte actually developed the "dialectical process" before Georg Hegel to whom this process is attributed. Terry Pinkard in *Hegel: A Biography* (2001), revealed that Hegel was mentored by Illuminati member Jacob Abel (code name "Pythagoras Abderites").

Terry Melanson of the online Illuminati Conspiracy Archive (a website with extensive research information) indicated that "one of the core concepts that influenced him [Hegel] was the notion of a single 'philosophy of history.'" And according to Reinhart Koselleck in *Critique and Crisis: Enlightenment and the Modern Society* (1988), this philosophy "substantiated the elitist consciousness of the

Enlightenment. This was the power that the Illuminati possessed, a power they shared with the whole of the Enlightenment. This was the threat: it revealed the plan of conquest to those under attack." As Antony Sutton explained in *America's Secret Establishment: An Introduction to the Order of Skull & Bones*: "Progress in the Hegelian State is through contrived conflicts: the clash of opposites makes for progress. If you can control the opposite, you dominate the nature of the outcome." Remember here that the PE and Skull & Bones member William Whitney in the late nineteenth century devised a political strategy of giving large sums of money to both major political parties, and then alternating power so the public thinks it has a choice when both major political parties' candidates actually are controlled by the PE.

In John Robison's *Proofs of a Conspiracy* (1798), there is an entire section on both the French Revolution and German Union. At the end of his book are Robison's "General Reflections" wherein he said he was "eager to find out any remains of Weishaupt's Association. I was not surprised when I saw marks of its interference in the French Revolution.—In hunting for clearer proofs I found out the German Union—and, in fine, the whole appeared to be one great and wicked project, fermenting and working all over Europe."

In addition to historically prominent people such as Hegel being mentored by the Illuminati, there were several historically prominent people who themselves were members of The Order. For example, according to Hermann Schuttler in *Die Mitglieder des Illuminatenordens 1776-1787/93*, the father of modern educational theory and practice, Johann Heinrich Pestalozzi (code name "Alfred") founded a branch of the Illuminati in Zurich, Switzerland, in 1783. Schuttler also revealed that, surprisingly, Jesuit archbishop Karl Theodor Dalberg (arch-chancellor of the Holy Roman Empire) became an Illuminatus Major in July 1783, and was initiated into the highest degree of Magus or Philosopher in 1784. And according to Schuttler, perhaps the most famous of the Illuminati was the novelist and playwright Johann Goethe (code name "Abaris"), who in February 1783 was probably brought into the Order by Johann Bode (mentioned earlier).

Librarian of Congress (and Rhodes scholar) James Billington in *Fire in the Minds of Men* (1980), claims that Bode was also the "decisive channel of Illuminist influence" on revolutionary Nicholas Bonneville during his "first two visits to Paris [June of 1787]." Another famous individual influenced by the Illuminati was poet Percy Bysshe Shelley who on March 2, 1811, wrote a letter to the editor of the *Examiner* indicating he wanted "to form a methodical society" and asserted that people should "bear in mind the very great influence which, for years since, was gained by Illuminism."

Terry Melanson of the online Illuminati Conspiracy Archive claims that "a direct line of influence from the Illuminati to the French Revolution to the communist League of the Just is realized" in Filippo Michele Buonarroti. Although there is some debate as to whether Buonarroti joined an Illuminus lodge in 1786, he was definitely connected with important members of the Order. Furthermore, he was a strong proponent of the French Revolution, having Rousseau as his "master," as he would later write, and establishing educational institutions that promoted the socialism of Rousseau's *Social Contract*. J. L. Talmon in *The Rise of Totalitarian Democracy* (1952) adds that "Buonarroti entered into close relations with the [French Revolution] Jacobin leaders and was a frequent guest at Robespierre's lodgings . . . he [subsequently] joined the Conspiracy of Babeuf as one of its chiefs. After having served his prison sentence and gone into exile, he became the high priest of egalitarian Communism in Europe."

Buonarroti settled in Geneva in 1806, and was initiated into the Grand Orient Lodge of Des Amis Sincères. He organized many secret societies, the most important of which was the Sublimes Maîtres Parfaits. And according to Elizabeth Eisenstein in *The First Professional Revolutionist: Filippo Michele Buonarroti (1761-1837)*: "In its structure, as well as its gradualist aim, the Sublimes Maîtres

Parfaits resembled the order founded by Weishaupt in 1776." This is a critical point to remember. Although the original Illuminati no longer exists, it was continued in "structure and aim" by others after Weishaupt.

Buonarroti infiltrated the Italian Carbonari, which was later led by revolutionary Giuseppe Mazzini in the mid-nineteenth century. From 1824 to 1830 Buonarroti lived in Brussels and wrote Babeuf's *Conspiracy of Equals* (shortened translated title), which was read by Karl Marx and Friedrich Engels. The latter two were paid by the League of the Just to write the *Communist Manifesto* (1848). And this was at a time when a young John Ruskin (who has a swastika on his gravestone) had just completed his own education at Oxford University, where in the mid-1870s he would teach a young Cecil Rhodes.

According to award-winning author Alan Axelrod (a consultant to the Strong Museum in New York and the Henry Francis du Pont Winterthur Museum in Delaware) in his book *The International Encyclopedia of Secret Societies and Fraternal Orders* (1997), Ruskin was "reputedly a student of the ILLUMINATI." And pertaining to Rhodes, in Will Banyan's "A Short History of the Round Table—Part I" there is a section called "The New Weishaupt" about Rhodes. In 1891, Cecil Rhodes formed the Secret Society of the Elect "to take the government of the whole world," in Rhodes' own words.

Also in the 1870s, Wilhelm Wundt established the first laboratory in experimental psychology at the University of Leipzig. Wundt's grandfather, Kirchenrat Karl Kasimir Wundt, was a member of the Illuminati (code name "Raphael"), according to the "Illuminati Provincial Report" from Utica dated September 1782 (see Richard van Dulmen's *Der Geheimbund Der Illuminatum*, and a good source for original Illuminati documents is www.bavarian-illuminati.info).

That Wilhelm Wundt's grandfather was a member of the Order, of course, doesn't guarantee the grandson was an adherent of the Illuminati's principles. However, it is noteworthy that the "Father of

Progressive Education," John Dewey, was a co-author and signer of the first *Humanist Manifesto* (1933), and Dewey's mentor, G. Stanley Hall, was the first of Wilhelm Wundt's American students.

The *Humanist Manifesto*'s principle that ethics are autonomous and situational is basically the same as Illuminati founder Weishaupt's principle of "Do what thou wilt." And the values of secular humanism have been taught in American public schools for at least the last fifty years.

Shortly before Cecil Rhodes attended Oxford and Wundt set up his laboratory in Leipzig, another individual like Weishaupt who believed in liberty of thought was Albert Pike. In 1871, Pike authored *Morals and Dogma*, in which he explained: "Everything scientific and grand in the dreams of the Illuminati, Jacob Boehme, Swedenborg, Saint-Martin, and others, is borrowed from the Kabalah. . . . Liberty of thought . . . universal Fraternity! A new doctrine, a new religion. . . ."

Pike praised Lucifer as the light-bearer, as did Alice Bailey whose works were first published in the early twentieth century by Lucifer Publishing. In *A Treatise on the Seven Rays: Esoteric Psychology* (1936 and 1942), she described the goals and characteristics of what she called "the Illuminati of the world." To Bailey, this Illuminati was comprised of the enlightened ones, people enlightened by Lucifer. And Bailey emphasized the need for a "new world order" and "points of light" connected to "service," just as President George H. W. Bush later did in his presidency.

But before having a global "new world order," a reshaping of America into President Lyndon Johnson's "Great Society" had to occur. Given the terms "great society" and "new world order" (a type of global great society), the latter of which would be characterized by a diminished national patriotism, is it purely coincidental that in John Robison's *Proofs of a Conspiracy* (1798) about the Illuminati, he related that once one became an Illuminatus Minor "the pupil is . . . convinced that it is a possible thing to unite all the inhabitants of the earth in one great society. . . . [Then] it may frequently be no hard task to make him think that patriotism is a narrow-minded monopolizing sentiment." This would enable the Illuminati to "rule the world," a purpose of the Order according to Robison.

While many people understand that the Illuminati existed and may have dispersed throughout Europe, they doubt that the Order came to America. However, in Augustin Barruel's *Memoirs Illustrating the History of Jacobinism* (1798) there is a joint juridical deposition by former Illuminati members Joseph Utzschneider, Georg Grunberger, and Johann Cosandey before Elector Karl Theodor (September 9, 1785) in which they indicated they were informed by several of their "Brethren" that "this Sect [the Illuminati] under different names has already spread itself in Italy, . . . in Austria, in Holland, in Saxony, on the Rhine, . . . and even as far as America."

Edmond Charles (Citizen) Genet spent a good deal of time at the Lodge of the Nine Sisters in Paris which was frequented by the Illuminati. In 1793, he became French envoy to the U.S., and then set up "Democratic Societies" such as the Mingo Creek Democratic Society in western Pennsylvania that fomented the Whiskey Rebellion of July 1794 (they actually wanted to secede and set up their own country there). President George Washington considered Genet a threat to the U.S. and asked him to leave the country. Washington later (October 24, 1798) wrote a letter to Rev. G. W. Snyder (see next page) expressing his concern over the influence of the Illuminati in America, stating: "It was not my intention to doubt that the doctrines of the Illuminati . . . had not spread in the United States. On the contrary, no one is more truly satisfied of this fact than I am." You can see the original handwritten letter in the "American Memory" section of the Library of Congress website.

Earlier that year, on May 9, 1798, in Charlestown, South Carolina (where Citizen Genet originally landed on April 8, 1793), Rev. Jedediah Morse preached the following:

> Practically all of the civil and ecclesiastical establishments of Europe

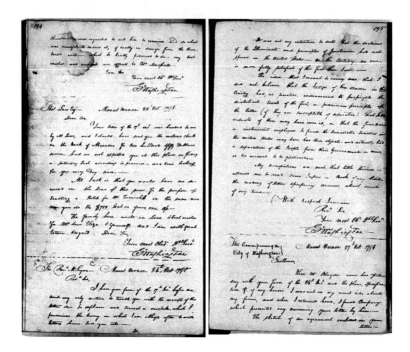

The October 24, 1798, letter from George Washington to Rev. G. W. Snyder

have already been shaken to their foundations by this terrible organization [the Illuminati]; the French Revolution itself is doubtless to be traced to its machinations.... The Jacobins are nothing more nor less than the open manifestation of the hidden system of the Illuminati. The Order has its branches established and its emissaries at work in America. The affiliated Jacobin societies in America have doubtless had as the object of their establishment the propagation of the principles of the illuminated mother club in France.

Then, less than two months later on July 4, 1798, Dr. Timothy Dwight, president of Yale University, delivered a discourse in which he claimed:

> In the societies of Illuminati doctrines were taught . . . [such as]: The being of God was denied and ridiculed; . . . the possession of property was pronounced to be robbery; . . . adultery, assassination,

poisoning, and other crimes of the like infernal nature, were taught as lawful, and even as virtuous actions. To crown such a system of falsehood and horror all means were declared to be lawful, provided the end was good. . . . Of the goodness of the end every man is to judge for himself. . . . The great and good ends proposed by the Illuminati . . . are the overthrow of religion, government, and human society civil and domestic. These they pronounce to be so good, that murder . . . and war, however extended and dreadful, are declared by them to be completely justifiable, if necessary for these great purposes. . . . With unremitted ardor and diligence the members insinuated themselves into every place of power and trust, and into every literary, political and friendly society; engrossed as much as possible the education of youth, especially of distinction; became licensers of the press, and directors of every literary journal; . . . enlisted in their service almost all the booksellers, and of course the printers, of Germany; . . . panegyrized and trumpeted those of themselves and their coadjutors; . . . In the private papers, seized in the custody of the leading members of Germany, several such societies [of the Illuminati] are recorded as having been erected in America, before the year 1786.

The threat of the Illuminati's philosophy was especially felt in Pennsylvania after the Whiskey Rebellion to such an extent that the president of the County Courts of the Fifth Circuit, Alexander Addison, felt the need to present "A Charge to the Grand Juries" of those courts' December 1800 sessions titled "Rise and Progress of Revolution." In this presentation, Addison referred to a "Conspiracy to destroy the principles which adorn, support, and connect civil society, and to bring men back to the savage state of Nature. Such was the object of the Illuminees or the Illuminati . . . with the daring ambition of governing the whole world. . . . All Government . . . was to be abolished; that an absolute and despotic tyranny might be exercised over the whole earth. . . . Have we no fear that a similar [to Europe] conspiracy exists here?" Addison concluded by asserting that the spirit of Illuminati "seems to exist in America . . . by the same means, by secret societies, by the press, by occupying publications and places of instruction. . . . That the press is used . . . will not be doubted by any who see the unprincipled similarity of publications." It is noteworthy here to mention that Cecil Rhodes' Secret Society of the Elect's purpose was "to take the government of the whole world," and with J. P. Morgan's money buy control of America's newspapers.

When President Washington asked Illuminist Citizen Genet to leave the United States as French envoy to America, he did it via his secretary of state, Thomas Jefferson. Genet expressed surprise that Jefferson would do this, and he reminded Jefferson in a letter that it was he (Jefferson) who had "initiated me [Genet] in the mysteries" that influenced Genet's hatred of those seeking absolute power (including religious).

Jefferson was an apologist for Illuminati founder Adam Weishaupt, and in a January 31, 1800, letter to Rev. James Madison, Jefferson said: "Weishaupt seems to be an enthusiastic Philanthropist. He is among those who believe in the indefinite perfectibility of man. . . . Weishaupt believes that to promote this perfection of the human character was the object of Jesus Christ." In this letter, Jefferson said he has just seen the third volume of Abbe Barruel's *Antisocial Conspiracy*. He also mentions "Robinson's" (sic) work concerning Weishaupt and the Illuminati as well as Rev. Jedediah Morse's, and he refers to them as "the ravings" of all three men.

Perhaps Jefferson's deism affected his attitude toward Weishaupt, because in 1802 John Wood authored *A Full Exposition of the Clintonian Faction and the Society of the Columbian Illuminati* concerning the establishment of the Theistical Society in America:

> For the avowed purpose of propagating Deism and opposing Christian religion. . . . It arose . . . in the same manner as the Illuminati originated . . . [and] after the example of the Illuminati

were divided into three or more grades. . . . The grand literary journal set in motion by the Columbian Illuminati was the Temple of Reason. . . . Another great point in the Theistical Society of New York, in common with the Illuminati of Germany, was to endeavor, if possible, to get all the public offices in the United States, filled with Deists. . . . The oath taken by the directors of the highest grade [of the Theistical Society] was nearly the same as the oath administered to the minerval among the Illuminati, . . . and must, without doubt, have been copied from it.

It was reported to me in these words—"I, a member of the Theistical Society, protest before you, the worthy President of our order, that I acknowledge my natural weakness and inability. . . . I bind myself to perpetual silence and unshaken loyalty, in submission to the order, in the person of our President, here making a faithful and complete surrender of my private judgments, my own will, and every narrow minded employment of my power and influence. I pledge myself to account the good of the order as my own, and am ready to serve it with my fortune, my honour and my blood." . . . By means of a corresponding committee, similar societies were established in different cities of America. Their principles in politics corresponded to their ideas of religion, viz. the rankest jacobinism, with the vilest deism. They all attached themselves to the interest of Mr. DeWitt Clinton. . . . He has been the means of displacing several worthy Christians to make way for them; and he bestows in bountiful measure all his patronage toward their political paper, The American Citizen. Nothing can prove more distinctly the mutual affection and sympathy which exist between Mr. Clinton and the Columbian Illuminati than these acts of kindness.

Dewitt Clinton was the nephew of Gov. George Clinton, who was the vice president of Thomas Jefferson (Weishaupt apologist) from 1805 to 1809. And Illuminist Citizen Genet married Governor Clinton's daughter Cornelia Clinton.

The seriousness of the Illuminati threat in America was explained ten years later in a July 4 sermon by Pastor Joseph Willard in a church in Lancaster, New Hampshire, when he claimed:

> There is sufficient evidence that a number of Societies of the illuminati, have been established in this land.... They are, doubtless, secretly striving to undermine all our ancient institutions, civil and sacred.... We live in an alarming period. The enemies of all order are seeking our ruin. Should infidelity generally prevail, our independence would fall, of course. Our republican government will be annihilated.

It's not just that the Illuminati's influence in America was occurring via religious societies and placing philosophical supporters in government offices, but the seedbed for creating a societal change was occurring via the schools. According to Will Monroe's *History of the Pestalozzian Movement in the United States* (1907), the educational ideas of the Illuminati member Johann Pestalozzi (code name "Alfred") began to be printed in journals and textbooks in the U.S. in 1806 and began to be used in some school systems, especially in New England where they would be viewed favorably by the intelligentsia of Horace Mann's day. This was the first half of the 1800s, and Mann became known as the "Father of American Public Education." Lawrence Cremin in *Transformation of the School* (1961) said: "For Mann the essence of the moral act was free self-choice." This was also a belief of Weishaupt.

According to Terry Melanson of Illuminati Conspiracy Archive, utopian socialist Robert Owen visited Illuminist Pestalozzi

> at Yverdon, Switzerland in 1818 and applied Pestalozzianism in Britain and America. Originally from Scotland, Owen used the word "socialist" in print (1827) for the first time, organized the first socialist movement in England (1835), and eventually

was venerated as the "patriarch of English Communism." . . . He influenced the likes of Etienne Cabet (1788–1856) and Goodwyn Barmby, both founding fathers of communism; . . . and, perhaps most importantly, Friedrich Engels (1820–1895) and Karl Marx (1818–1883), authors of *The Communist Manifesto* [in 1848].

In Illuminati founder Adam Weishaupt's instructions to those of the degree of Epopts, he says the Illuminizing Legislator states: "You will incessantly form new plans, and try every means . . . to seize upon the public education, the ecclesiastical government, the chairs of literature, and the pulpit." Specifically concerning public education, in the "continuation of the Instructions on the Government of the Illuminees—Laws for the Local Superiors," one finds the following:

> Our strength chiefly consists in numbers; but much will also depend on the means employed to form the pupil—Young people are pliant and easily take the impression.—The Prefect will therefore spare no pains to gain possession of the *Schools* which lie within his district, and also of their teachers. He will find need of placing them under the tuition of members of our Order; for this is the true method of infusing our principles and of training our young men: it is thus that the most ingenious men are prepared to labour for us and are brought into discipline; and thus that the affection conceived by our young pupils for the Order will gain as deep root as to all other early impressions.

Establishing the first commune in the U.S. in 1825 at New Harmony, Indiana, Robert Owen in his opening address claimed: "I am come to this country to introduce an entire new order of society; to change it from an ignorant selfish system, to an enlightened social system, which shall gradually unite all interests into one and remove all cause for contest between individuals."

Joining Owen at New Harmony in 1828 was Frances Wright

(formerly Madame Francoise d'Arusmont, brought to the U.S. by the Marquis de Lafayette) who, with Owen's son Robert Dale Owen and Orestes Brownson, formed The Workingmen's Party in New York. After Brownson converted to Christianity, he later revealed in *The Works of Orestes Brownson* that their plan in establishing their political party was as follows:

> The great object was to get rid of Christianity, and to convert our churches into halls of science. The plan was not to make open attacks on religion, although we might belabor the clergy and bring them into contempt where we could; but to establish a system of state,—we said national—schools from which all religion was to be excluded, in which nothing was to be taught but such knowledge as is verifiable by the senses, and to which all parents were to be compelled by law to send their children. Our complete plan was to take the children from their parents at the age of twelve or eighteen months, and to have them nursed, fed, clothed, and trained in these schools at the public expense; but at any rate, we were to have godless schools for all the children of the country.... The plan has been successfully pursued,... and the whole action of the country on the subject has taken the direction we sought to give it.... One of the principal movers of the scheme had no mean share in organizing the Smithsonian Institute....

This fit well within Weishaupt's educational plan.

Relevant to "schools from which all religion was to be excluded," in the early 1960s Bible reading and school prayer were banned by the U.S. Supreme Court. Relevant to only "knowledge as is verifiable by the senses" being taught, this was promoted by teaching exclusively Darwinian evolution. Relevant to children "at the age of twelve or eighteen months" being "nursed, fed, clothed and trained" in public schools, Lamar Alexander (who would become U.S. Secretary of Education) on November 1, 1989, referred to "schools [that] will serve children from age three months" to age eighteen. And relevant to "godless schools for all the children of the country," William Z. Foster (head of the American Communist Party) in *Toward Soviet America* (1932) referred to "studies being cleansed of religious features" and said "God will be banished . . . from the schools."

Another area in which one can see the lineage of Weishaupt's "Do what thou wilt" philosophy can be seen in abortion. Earlier I mentioned that Weishaupt and his sister-in-law "tried every method in our power to destroy the child" in her womb. Weishaupt believed that his Illuminati elite should rule over the people. The Order influenced the French Revolution, and one of the revolution's elite "philosopher kings" was the Marquis de Sade (from whom the word "sadist" comes). In de Sade's *La Philosophie Dans le Boudoir* (1795), he said it was necessary to utilize induced abortion for social reasons to control the population. This view can be seen in the twentieth century in Planned Parenthood founder Margaret Sanger's view that abortion could be used to lessen the number of "dysgenic stock," whom she believed included "Jews, Catholics, Negroes and Gypsies" among others.

More recently, the eugenic or population control aspect of abortion can be seen in a letter by James B. Hunt, Jr. when he was governor of North Carolina. He was asked why he supported tax funding of abortions, and he replied that it was because "we must concentrate on raising new generations of children who aren't stunted or handicapped in some way." Remember, he was not talking about contraception, but rather about paying women for their abortions (killings) after their children have been conceived.

At the level of higher education, the Illuminati had formed student societies at universities, for example in Germany at Tugenbund and Burschenschaften. William H. Russell matriculated through those institutions, and brought back the student societies' ceremonies and rites to Yale University, establishing the secretive Skull & Bones (S&B) society there in the early 1830s. S&B acknowledges today that it came "from the German chapter," which presented as a gift to S&B a painting that seems to depict the rites of the Regent degree of the Illuminati. Moreover, Laurence Sterne's *The Life and Opinions of Tristram Shandy, Gentleman* was recommended reading for Illuminati initiates. One of the most important characters in this book is "Uncle Toby," which is also the name of the most important figure during S&B initiations.

S&B has focused on preparing an elite, just as the Illuminati focused on preparing "the most ingenious men." As for others, Clarence Karier in *The Individual, Society, and Education: A History of American Educational Ideas* (1986) wrote that Illuminist Pestalozzi "argued for a practical education for the new proletariat and was looked upon with favor by the power elite for suggesting that 'the poor must be educated for poverty' for in order 'to enjoy the best possible state, both of soul and body . . . it is necessary to desire and be content with still less.'" This is very similar to the view of Frederick Gates, the head of Rockefeller's General Education Board founded in 1902. Gates in *Occasional Letter, No. 1* revealed that, "In our dream, we have limitless resources, and the people yield themselves with perfect docility to our molding hand. The present educational conventions fade from our minds; and, unhampered by tradition, we work our own good will upon a grateful and responsive rural folk."

The values taught in public schools today also flow from Weishaupt's principle of "Do what thou wilt." German historian Reinhart Koselleck put Weishaupt "in a row with [Comte Henri de] Saint-Simon and [Karl] Marx." From 1818 to 1824, Saint-Simon's secretary was Auguste Comte, who from 1851 to 1857 wrote a four-volume set titled *System of Positive Polity* explaining his "Positive Philosophy" in which collective humanity became more important than the individual, and it replaced God as the focus of worship.

This positivist philosophy was perhaps the origin of the modern secular humanist movement. John Dewey, the "Father of Progressive Education," was a signer of the first *Humanist Manifesto* (1933) which declared that values are autonomous and situational. Another signer, Charles Francis Potter, in *Humanism: A New Religion* (1930) proclaimed: "Education is thus a most powerful ally of humanism. What can the theistic Sunday schools, meeting for an hour once a week, and teaching only a fraction of the children, do to stem the tide of a five-day program of humanistic teaching?"

Fourteen years later, the head of the World Health Organization, Brock Chisholm, in the February 1946 edition of *Psychiatry* expressed his desire for a world government and that children should be world citizens. Then he wrote:

> We have swallowed all manner of poisonous certainties fed us by our parents, our Sunday and day school teachers, our politicians, our priests.... The reinterpretation and eventual eradication of the concept of right and wrong which has been the basis of child training, the substitution of intelligent and rational thinking for faith in the certainties of the old people, these are the belated objectives ... for charting the changes in human behavior.

Remember that Adam Weishaupt wanted to do away with moral absolutes, and his second-in-command of the Illuminati, Baron von Knigge (mentioned at the beginning of this chapter), wanted to create "world citizens."

Twenty-four years after Chisholm's article was published, leading educator Ted Sizer in *Five Lectures . . . On Moral Education* (1970) declared that "Moral autonomy ... is the 'new morality' toward which we are to guide ourselves and other people." Then in the September/October 1981 edition of *The Humanist,* H. J. Blackham (a founder of the 4 million-member International Humanist and Ethical Union) wrote that if schools teach dependence (moral, etc.) on oneself, "they are more revolutionary than any conspiracy to overthrow the government." Unfortunately, he was absolutely right!

I have already mentioned that the Illuminati had spread to the

U.S. in the late eighteenth century and was recognized as a dangerous force here. In "An Oration Delivered at Byfield" by Rev. Elijah Parish, A.M., on July 4, 1799, he opined:

> It was reserved for Weishaupt, whose name would figure in a biography of Devils, to organize a society to overturn all the governments and religions of the world: A society, which for depravity of design and address in execution, far exceeds any scheme of Lucifer, any plot of rebellion conceived in the councils of hell: A society, which would indubitably place its author first in the catalogue of the damned, were he not rivaled in impiety by d'Alembert, Frederic and Voltaire. They taught that conjugal faithfulness, chastity and all the moral virtues, were mere prejudices of education; that modesty was refined voluptuousness; that self-murder was no crime; that the possession of property infringed on human rights, that the motive justifies the means; that civil government is the only fall of man; that there is no future state—no God. These opinions are propagated over countries, inhabited by more than a hundred million souls. The apostles of these doctrines introduced each other into every department of the community.
>
> They sat in the reviewers chair; they guided the public taste for books; they taught in the schools; they lectured in the universities; they prescribed to the sick; they were the tutors of Princes; they hovered round the throne, and directed the sceptre. To finish this climax of guilt they ascended to the Pulpit, and with unhallowed lips, perverted the truth, and polluted the pages of God. This society, after extending itself through Germany, Holland, Switzerland, and Italy, was formally introduced to Paris, to all France. . . . Their secret papers have been discovered, which prove there are 2660 of these lodges in the world; seventeen of which are in the United States. How many more there may be, it is not easy to conjecture. . . . "Satan, when seeking vengeance against his divine creator, would have been proud to become the pupil of this modern Spartacus."

> ... When in 1798 all places of christian worship were abolished in Paris, the nations of christendom were shocked.

Why were they shocked? It was because in 1794 the public was informed that from 1790, "every concern of the Illuminees had ceased." This is according to *Proofs of the Real Existence, and Dangerous Tendency, of Illuminism* (1802) by Seth Payson, A.M., who also explained that "in 1791, a spark of Illuminism caught in Ireland, and spread with astonishing rapidity, threatening a universal conflagration."

Robespierre during the French Revolution wanted to crush the rival Brissotine faction, and he therefore criticized Citizen Genet of that faction who supported Illuminist principles and came to the United States in 1793 as French envoy, landing at Charlestown, South Carolina, where Seth Payson's book was published. Robespierre commented, "Genet, their [Brissotine faction] agent at Philadelphia, made himself chief of a club there, and never ceased to make and excite motions equally injurious and perplexing to the government."

Earlier in this chapter, I mentioned that Thomas Jefferson was an apologist for Weishaupt and a friend of Genet, and the seriousness of the threat the Illuminati posed to the U.S. can be seen in a June 30, 1813, letter John Adams wrote to Jefferson dramatically stating: "You certainly never felt the Terrorism, created by Genet, in 1793, when ten thousand People in the Streets of Philadelphia, day after day, threatened to drag Washington out of his House, and effect a Revolution in the government, or compel it to declare War in favour of the French Revolution, and against England."

Concerning the effect of the Illuminati even after it disbanded, Seth Payson explained: "Admitting that the order of the Illuminees is now extinct, their systems and doctrines remain; the books by which they communicated their poison are in circulation; the arts by which they inveigled and corrupted the minds of men are not forgotten, and the former members of this society still possess the skill, the wicked subtlety to which the care of Weishaupt formed his adepts."

I related that Thomas Jefferson was an apologist for Illuminati founder Adam Weishaupt, calling him in 1800 simply "an enthusiastic Philanthropist." However, in professor of divinity David Tappan's "A Discourse Delivered in the Chapel of Harvard College, June 19, 1798," he explained that the Illuminati operated only "under the mask of universal philanthropy."

Tappan further remarked:

> But what connection had this German association with the Revolution and consequent measures of France? The answer is, the secret papers of the society prove that it had extended its branches into the latter country before the year 1786; that Mirabeau and Talleyrand, two distinguished agents in that revolution, were officers of a secret lodge at Paris in 1788; that during the sitting of the Notables in that year deputies were sent to France from the German Illuminati, at the request of this lodge, to aid in the projected subversion of religion and government. . . . The German agents, on their arrival, persuaded lodges to form a political committee, whose object should be to devise the best means for a general revolution. From these committees arose the famous Jacobin Club, whose primary aim was to revolutionize not only France, but, if possible, the world.

Tappan then explained that "The supposition of some deep and extensive a conspiracy against government and religion . . . easily accounts for . . . certain newspapers and other productions . . . which aim or direfully tend to undermine the religious and moral, as well as civil institutions, principles and habits of our country. . . ."

Earlier I described the connections between the Illuminati and Yale University's secret society Skull & Bones (to which both Presidents Bush belonged) founded in 1832. On the front page of the National Research Institute's *Trumpet* (October 1988), one reads: "Toward the end of the ceremony of initiation into the 'Regents Degree of Illuminism,' according to a tract, 'A skeleton is pointed out to him (the initiate), at the feet of which are laid a crown and a sword. He is asked whether that is the skeleton of a king, a nobleman, or a beggar.'"

According to Ron Rosenbaum in his article, "Last Secrets of Skull and Bones" (*Esquire*, September 1977), this statement is quite similar to the words (in German), "Who was the fool, who was the wise man, beggar, or king? Whether poor or rich, all's the same in death," which appears above a painting of skulls in Room 322 of Skull & Bones.

Nine years after Skull & Bones was founded, President Franklin Roosevelt ancestor and New York assemblyman Clinton Roosevelt (CR) authored *The Science of Government Founded in Natural Law* (1841). CR, like New York governor DeWitt Clinton, was reportedly a member of the Columbian Lodge of the Order of the Illuminati. And similar to Weishaupt's philosophy, in CR's book the assemblyman wrote: "There is no God of justice to order things aright on earth; if there be a God, he is a malicious and vengeful being, who created us for misery." CR referred to other members of his "order" as "the enlightened ones" (the Illuminees).

Given the horrible reputation of the Illuminati, one might wonder why George W. Bush in his A.D. 2000 presidential campaign would have Illuminati Online as his campaign's web server. This was after the president of Illuminati Online, Steve Jackson, developed a card game in 1994 called "Illuminati: New World Order" with a supplement called "Assassins" (see www.cuttingedge.org/news/n1753.cfm). One of the cards in the card game shows one of the Twin Towers of the World Trade Center in New York City being hit by a terrorist attack, and another card shows the Pentagon partly in flames from an attack.

One of the first major pieces of legislation George W. Bush supported was the No Child Left Behind Act of 2001, which placed the Center for Civic Education (CCE) in charge of developing civic education for all of America's schools. CCE viewed its role as "to improve our curricular frameworks and standards for a world transformed by globally accepted and internationally transcendent principles." In that regard, CCE's textbook, *We the People*, on page 202 states: "The culture we live in is becoming cosmopolitan, that is, belonging to the whole world."

The use of the word "cosmopolitan" is of special interest because in ex-Illuminatus Ernst von Gochhausen's novel *Exposure of the Cosmopolitan System: In Letters from ex-Freemasons* (1786), one reads: "The hero asked his superior very frankly, 'What purposes do the Illuminati have in infiltrating and now dominating Masonry?' The reply was blunt and simple: 'To emancipate all of mankind from religious and political slavery. Put specifically, to advance deism and cosmopolitanism.'... World citizenship. What does it mean? You are either a citizen [of the world] or you are a rebel. There is no third choice."

This is the future the Illuminati and Power Elite have planned for us. In Berlin on July 24, 2008, presidential candidate Barack Obama not only said he was a "proud citizen of the United States," but also a "fellow citizen of the world." The word "citizen" as opposed to "resident" or "inhabitant" has legal implications. And if there is a conflict between national citizenship and world citizenship, guess which one takes precedence? It would be world citizenship, just like in the U.S. it is federal law that takes precedence over state law.

On the night of January 15, 2011, during the Miss America Pageant, Miss Hawaii was the first finalist to be asked a question by the judges. She was asked whether she considered herself first a citizen of her state, of the country, or of the world. Predictably, she replied that she considered herself first a "citizen of the world." Evidently, this is more important to her than being a citizen of the United States. And earlier the same day that she made her declaration, the American radio broadcast of Duke University's basketball game was in Mandarin Chinese, a first in sports broadcast history and, no doubt, completely acceptable for those conditioned to be "citizens of the world."

# The Psychological Conditioning of Americans

In the past, I have mentioned that Edward Bernays in *Propaganda* (1928) said: "Those who manipulate the organized habits and opinions of the masses constitute an invisible government which is the true ruling power of the country.... The technical means have been invented and developed by which opinion may be regimented." And in *The Impact of Science on Society* (1951), Bertrand Russell wrote: "Although this science of mass psychology will be diligently studied, it will be rigidly confined to the governing class. The populace will not be allowed to know how its convictions are generated."

In 1966, Dr. James McConnell, a professor of psychology at the University of Michigan, stated: "I teach a course called The Psychology of Influence, and I begin it by stating categorically that the time has come when, if you give me any normal human being and a couple of weeks, ... I can change his behavior from what it is not to whatever you want it to be, if it's physically possible.... I can turn him from a Christian into a communist and vice versa.... Look, we can do these things. We can control behavior."

Five years later, Milton Rokeach in "Persuasion That Persists" (*Psychology Today*, September 1971) proclaimed:

> Suppose you could take a group of people, give them a twenty-minute pencil-and-paper task, talk to them for ten to twenty minutes

afterward, and thereby produce long-range changes in core values and personal behavior in a significant portion of this group. For openers, it would of course have major implications for education, government, propaganda, and therapy. . . . My colleagues and I in the last five years achieved the kinds of results suggested in the first paragraph of this article. . . . It now seems to be within man's power to alter experimentally another person's basic values, and to control the direction of the change.

How did the psychological conditioning of Americans toward this end occur? In *Science of Coercion: Communication Research and Psychological Warfare 1945-1960* (1994), Christopher Simpson referred to

> the engineering of consent of targeted populations at home and abroad. . . . Various leaders in the social sciences engaged one another in tacit alliances to promote their particular interpretations of society. . . . They regarded mass communication as a tool for social management and as a weapon in social conflict. . . . Key academic journals of the day . . . concentrated on how modern technology could be used by elites to manage social change, extract political concessions, or win purchasing decisions from targeted audiences. . . . This orientation reduced the extraordinarily complex, inherently communal process of communication to simple models based on the dynamics of transmission of persuasive—and, in the final analysis, coercive—messages.

Sometimes, the messages have been subliminal, as Robert Bornstein in "Subliminal Techniques as Propaganda Tools" (*Journal of the Mind and Behavior*, Summer 1989) indicated that subliminal methods might be successfully used to deliver propaganda messages, because "the undetectable ability of subliminal stimuli may diminish their resistability relative to other persuasion techniques." In case one is skeptical as to whether subliminal techniques work, refer to a study by G. J. W. Smith, D. P. Spence, and G. S. Klein ("Subliminal Effects of Verbal Stimuli," *Journal of Abnormal and Social Psychology*, pages 167–176), which was described by them as follows:

> A static, expressionless portrait of a man was flashed on a screen by Smith, Spence and Klein. They requested their subjects to note how the expression of the picture changed. They intermittently flashed the word "angry" on the screen, at exposures so brief that the subjects were consciously completely unaware of having seen the word. They tended, however, to see the face as becoming more angry. When the word "happy" was flashed on the screen in similar fashion, the viewers tended to see the face as becoming more happy. Thus they were clearly influenced by stimuli which registered at a subliminal level, stimuli of which the individual was not, and could not, be aware.

Two years before the article by Smith, Spence, and Klein, *Battle for the Mind: The Mechanics of Indoctrination, Brainwashing, and Thought Control* by psychiatrist William Sargant was published, in which he indicated that if certain "underlying psychological principles are once understood, it should be possible to get at the person, converting and maintaining him in his new belief by a whole variety of imposed stresses that end by altering his brain function." Sargant further explained that the human brain "is particularly sensitive to rhythmic stimulation by percussion and bright lights. . . . Belief can be implanted in people after brain function has been sufficiently disturbed by . . . induced fear, anger or excitement. Of the results caused by such disturbances, the most common one is temporarily impaired judgment and heightened suggestibility."

Over twenty years ago, I wrote "Beware subliminal messages in media" in the *Orlando Sentinel* (July 22, 1990), and I am reproducing most of that article below, because it is still relevant to what I have written in the first part of this chapter. The article reads as follows:

Change is becoming an increasing part of American society. Business promotes changing styles to sell products. Social engineers are trying to change our values. There actually seems to be a "cult of change" today, as many individuals are always seeking something new and different.

Much of the stimuli for change has come through television, and there is already some research evidence that a number of people have engaged in violent behavior based upon the violence they saw on television. One wonders also how many might have been effected by messages such as "Read us any rule, we'll break it," in the theme for the television program "Laverne and Shirley"? And how many saw one of the first episodes of "Hardball" last season where the two police heroes tossed rocks at a streetlight just to see who would ride the bike, causing one of them to say, "Now we're lawbreakers"? Currently, there is an ad showing a child rigging a contraption to swipe his father's Eggo waffle, which certainly doesn't reinforce the biblical admonition, "Thou shalt not steal."

It's in this latter area of TV advertising that perhaps the most insidious threat comes, and it comes not just in the content of the ads, but in the method. You have probably noticed in the last couple of years that there have been an increasing number of commercials with flashing lights and quickly changing images. I asked a university professor of TV communications about this new type of hyper-reality that was being promoted. I thought one's natural inclination would be to turn away from that which is stressful to the eye, and I didn't see how that could help to sell a company's product. The professor explained that about four to five years ago, many of the people who had produced music videos had become involved in commercial advertising. A concept was developed that no longer appealed to the reasons viewers should buy a particular product, but rather through quick images showed a lifestyle with which a target audience associates.

What is at work in the mind of the viewer during these ads?

Well, the reason most people can fill in the blanks for "Things go better with ___" and "Have you driven a ___ lately?" is because they have seen those messages repeated over and over again in ads. Now, what if instead of stating a message just once in an ad, the message was flashed repeatedly in front of the viewer? Instead of just one mental image or imprint, there would be many. Also, whenever the eye sees quickly changing images, there is a tendency to try to focus one's concentration all the more. When the final message remains clearly on the screen, the mind in its relief at being given an unchanging image absorbs the final message more fully.

It is easy to see the tremendous and ominous potential that type of advertising can have in the form of mental conditioning or indoctrination, especially if the person's "will" can be controlled. In that regard, Professor Willis Harman of Stanford University's Engineering Economic Systems Department believes that a person's behavior is governed far more extensively than we realize by the unconscious or subconscious mind. Research has already shown that quick flashes of subliminal messages have been successfully used as conditioning or programming tools.

Research published about five years ago (about the same time as the new type of television ads began to appear) by Benjamin Libet, professor of neurophysiology at the University of California, San Francisco, in the scientific journal *The Brain and Behavioral Sciences*, indicates that "the conscious mind doesn't initiate voluntary actions." Monitors revealed that about a half-second before a muscle flexes, for example, an unconscious part of the brain sends signals seemingly to prepare the conscious part of the brain for action. Libet says the conscious part of the brain can veto the unconscious signal, but the question is, "What if the person's 'will' has been conditioned not to veto the signal?" What if the person has seen the Nike slogan "Just do it" so many times that he or she "just does it"—whatever it is?

What does "Just do it" mean? Is it like, "If it feels good, do it"?

After all, the commercial doesn't say, "Just buy Nike." Usually people say, "Just do it" when they are advising someone to stop thinking about the pros and cons of some value judgment or when they are ordering someone to do something. In a landmark trial that began in Reno, Nevada, the rock group Judas Priest is alleged to have a subliminal message, "Do it, do it," on their album "Stained Glass," which supposedly led to the suicides of two teens who chanted "Do it, do it, do it" before they shot themselves after hearing the album. One of the teens survived long enough to say it was as though the music controlled his actions, leaving him without a free will, and, "It was like a self-destruct that went off. We had been programmed."

Dr. Robert Assagioli, the founder of psychosynthesis, believes it is actually possible to train the "will," and if one can gradually condition the "will" by TV ads, then "Brave New World" here we come. Our freedom will be lost to indoctrination before most people aren't even aware of what is happening to them, and this should be a cause of great concern to all Americans.

The other day, someone asked me what the repetitious sound was they were hearing on a TV ad. I said it was what Bertrand Russell referred to as a sound "repeatedly intoned" used to condition or program people as part of a mass psychology means of control. The idea was that just as the repeatedly intoned sound would remain in the listener's mind, so too would the accompanying message, thereby making the sponsor's product more likely to be purchased by the listener!

Another favorite psychological technique the PE employs to control the masses is using crises and the public response to them to further the PE's objectives. For example, after the terrorist attacks of September 11, 2001, the public desired greater security, so the PE was ready to provide the Patriot Act and Homeland Security Act which eroded our freedoms (a goal of the PE).

# The Power Elite's Use of Misdirection

One of the primary mechanisms used by the Power Elite (PE) over the centuries to accomplish its goals is misdirection. For example, many people have been misdirected into believing the American Civil War was fought over the existence of slavery in the South. Actually, only about seven percent of Southerners owned slaves at the time of the war, but in one of my earlier NewsWithViews columns, and in my book *The Power Elite and the Secret Nazi Plan*, I relate the PE's tactic of promoting an issue (abolition of slavery) that would split the U.S. so the PE could create a Gulf Empire consisting of the Southern states along with Central America and the Caribbean islands.

In another NewsWithViews column, I described how the Cuban Missile Crisis was also an example of misdirection. In this case, the Soviets actually wanted us to see they had placed long-range nuclear missiles in Cuba so that we would demand their removal, and they would agree to comply in exchange for our assurance there would be no further attempts by us to invade Cuba. This guarantee would then enable them to use Cuba as a communist revolutionary training ground for Latin America (e.g., Nicaragua) and Africa (e.g., Angola).

In my book mentioned above, I described how Eleanor Dulles (the sister of Allen and John Foster Dulles) discovered information about Nelson Rockefeller working with the Nazis that was used to coerce him into agreeing to deliver the Latin American bloc of votes at the U.N. for the establishment of Israel in exchange for the Israelis not pursuing escaped Nazis after the Second World War. But do you really believe the Dulles brothers were so clumsy as to leave carelessly such information laying about for their sister to find? Perhaps this was actually an example of misdirection, and the guarantee of non-pursuit of Nazis after World War II was the goal all along, because such non-pursuit was critical to the fulfillment of the secret Nazi plan today.

At this point, it is important to remember that in the 1950s, Egyptian president Gamal Abdel Nasser discovered that the Muslim Brotherhood (MB), which had allied with the Nazis beginning in the 1930s, had been infiltrated by American and other intelligence agencies. Nasser (who was helped by over one hundred Nazi veterans subcontracted by the CIA) in 1957 said: "The genius of you Americans is that you never make clear cut stupid moves, only complicated stupid moves, which make us wonder at the possibility that there may be something we are missing." His suspicions were justified.

And to the extent the American government has been the primary enforcer of the PE's will over the last several decades, our suspicions are also justified regarding what the PE is doing today from North Africa to Afghanistan as part of the secret Nazi plan. Egyptian president Mohamed Morsi and Afghan president Hamid Karzai are puppets of the PE, just like American presidents have been for decades.

And so that the PE can "pull the strings" of its puppets, presidents have monitors. Just like Col. Edward M. House monitored the activities of President Woodrow Wilson, do you really believe Hillary Clinton just happened to meet Bill Clinton in the library at Yale University? Also, do you really believe Huma Abedin just happens to be Secretary of State Clinton's deputy chief-of-staff? Abedin has three family members associated with organizations having ties to the MB.

Likewise, do you really believe Valerie Jarrett just happens to be perhaps the closest adviser to President Obama? Jarrett was born in Iran in 1956 to a father who was in Iran from 1950 to 1961, which (perhaps coincidentally) includes the time the CIA was overthrowing

Iranian leader Mohammad Mossadegh (1953). Do you also believe PE agent Zbigniew Brzezinski just happens to be an adviser to President Obama? And Brzezinski, after advising President Jimmy Carter to support the Ayatollah Khomeini following the Shah's abdication in 1979, recently has been strongly advising President Obama *not* to take military action against Iran to prevent it from developing a nuclear weapon, even though Israel has informed him they believe their existence may depend upon such action.

I don't mention this out of a desire to see the ravages of war occur, but simply to show the extent of the PE's control. For the moment, at least, the PE simply doesn't want a major military conflict involving Iran. Iran is very important to the PE's secret plan, as in the 1930s the Shah of Iran admired Hitler so much that he changed his country's name in 1935 from Persia to Iran, which in Farsi means Aryan (in line with Hitler's concept of a superior Aryan race of people).

Recently, we might have seen another example of misdirection regarding who is to blame for the death of U.S. ambassador Chris Stevens and others in Benghazi, Libya. On the CBS Evening News (September 20, 2012), reporter Elizabeth Palmer indicated that the head of the Libyan government says Ansar al-Sharia was responsible. However, *Time* (September 24, 2012) said an al-Qaeda group called the Imprisoned Omar Abdul Rahman Brigades is responsible. The misdirection could be that if the former is responsible, the PE wants the latter blamed to distract from the former group's desire to implement sharia law far and wide. However, if the Rahman Brigades are responsible, the PE's misdirection would be to have al-Sharia blamed so President Obama would not be overly criticized if he releases Rahman (the blind sheikh imprisoned for the 1993 World Trade Center bombing) after the president's re-election (to satisfy new Egyptian president Mohamed Morsi's call for Rahman's release). On September 20, 2012, the *New York Post* reported U.S. Rep. Peter King confirmed that the Obama administration is considering a request from the Egyptian government that Rahman be released.

Although Mitt Romney is a puppet of the PE (if elected president, he would not have cancelled NAFTA, GATT, or Permanent Normal Trade Relations with Communist China), their preferred candidate for 2012 was puppet President Obama because of his Muslim background and movement of the U.S. toward socialism (e.g., taking over Fannie Mae, Freddie Mac, General Motors, etc.). For the PE, Mitt Romney was their Wendell Willkie of 2012 (Willkie was chosen by the PE to lose to President Roosevelt in 1940).

Therefore, it is important to note what Romney could have used against President Obama, but didn't. For example, Romney could have pounded the national airwaves with ads saying the Obama administration (especially Secretary of State Hillary Clinton) did not provide enough security for the U.S. ambassador and other Americans in Libya, but he didn't. Instead, President Obama was made to look like a macho commander-in-chief, sending the Marines to the region and demanding the Libyan perpetrators be brought to justice. Actually, U.S. Representative King mentioned above is chairman of the House Homeland Security Committee. On CNN, September 28, he said that Susan Rice's (U.S. ambassador to the U.N.) explanation of the Benghazi attack was "such a failure of foreign policy message and leadership" and "such a misstatement of facts" that "I believe she should resign." Susan Rice is a Rhodes scholar.

Also, a spokesman for the Libyan government telling Elizabeth Palmer on the September 20 CBS Evening News that his government wasn't yet strong enough to confront the alleged perpetrators could allow President Obama to insist the Marines be allowed to help the Libyan government in this task. And President Obama was made to look tough again when he told Egyptian president Morsi that he expected him to protect our government representatives in Egypt, and the MB there on September 14 suddenly transformed a large protest (supposedly over an American-made film denigrating Mohammed) into a small one.

The remainder of this chapter covers how the Power Elite (PE) uses misdirection in the form of reactions to crises to initiate wars, one of the favorite tactics of the PE in accomplishing its ultimate goal of world control. A useful starting point will be about one hundred years ago and the Spanish-American War. The impetus for the war was the misdirection of blame on Spain for the explosion of the battleship *Maine* on February 15, 1898. Later, it was discovered that the explosion was not from planted external charges, but rather from inside the U.S. battleship itself.

Regarding the First World War, its origin was due to the Austrian ultimatum (reaction) to Serbia over the assassination (crisis) of Archduke Franz Ferdinand on June 28, 1914. The misdirection occurred with British secretary of state Sir Edward Grey making statements to German ambassador to England Prince Karl Max Lichnowsky that didn't make it clear Britain would enter the conflict if Germany did.

The Second World War began with America declaring war (reaction) to the Japanese bombing of Pearl Harbor (crisis). And the Japanese attack upon Pearl Harbor was their "reaction" to the "crisis" of an American blockade and other actions against them. The misdirection was against the American people in that the attack upon Pearl Harbor was presented as a surprise, when President Roosevelt's actions intentionally provoked the Japanese attack, and FDR knew it was coming.

Similarly, the American people were misdirected into thinking our government supported the Nationalist Chinese, when actually Gen. George Marshall took measures to disarm them, thereby allowing the Communist Chinese to succeed in their revolution of 1949 (the PE would likewise support the communist revolution of Fidel Castro in Cuba in 1959). Thus, with Communist Chinese support, the North Koreans were able to stalemate the American-supported South Koreans in the Korean War of the early 1950s. This accomplished the PE objective of "no-win" wars as mentioned in Philip Freneau's essay in *American Museum* (July 1792) about the elite's strategy. This same "no-win" war strategy was followed in the 1960s and early 1970s by the Vietnam War, begun over the American "reaction" to the "crisis" of North Vietnamese PT boats attacking a U.S. destroyer on August 2, 1964, in the Gulf of Tonkin. Later, it was discovered the attack never occurred, as once again the American public had been misdirected.

The next major American conflict was in the 1991 Gulf War when the U.S. attacked Iraq. This misdirection was similar to that of the First World War, as April Glaspie, U.S. ambassador to Iraq, led Iraqi leader Saddam Hussein to believe his invasion of Kuwait would not be met with an American military response.

American (NATO) involvement in the Bosnian War of the late 1990s followed the pattern of World War II, as the U.S. "reacted" to the "humanitarian crisis" occurring in Kosovo. This "crisis" occurred, however, because Yugoslav leader Slobodan Milosevic was "reacting" to the "crisis" of Kosovo Liberation Army (KLA) terrorists inciting murder and chaos there. According to James Bissett, former Canadian ambassador to Yugoslavia, in "We Have Created a Monster" (*Toronto Globe and Mail*, July 31, 2001), the CIA (and British Special Armed Forces) armed and trained the KLA (in Albania) to foment revolution in Kosovo, which resulted in the assassination of Serbian mayors and ambush of Serbian police.

Similarly, the Iraq War of 2003 also followed the pattern of World War II. The American public was misdirected against Iraq after the U.S. attacked the Taliban in Afghanistan. This American military response was a "reaction" to the "crisis" of the September 11, 2001, attack upon the World Trade Center and Pentagon by al-Qaeda, which was harbored by the Taliban in Afghanistan.

And current news reports indicate that the U.S. (NATO) is considering helping NATO member Turkey, which is "reacting" to explosive shells from Syria falling upon Turkish land. This would, as in the case of Kosovo, give the U.S. (NATO) an excuse to respond to the "humanitarian crisis" occurring in Syria, as the forces of Syrian leader Hafez al-Assad "react" to the "crisis" of externally funded and armed revolutionaries within Syria trying to overthrow the government there.

# Oklahoma City Bombing Anniversary

In my last book, *The Power Elite and the Secret Nazi Plan,* I referred to infamous Nazi Adolph Eichmann associate Otto von Bolschwing, whom Allen Dulles (head of the CIA under President Eisenhower) helped immigrate to the U.S. in 1954. According to *The Secret War Against the Jews* by John Loftus and Mark Aarons, Bolschwing had said that in any future war, the support of the Muslim world was essential to Hitler's plan. Beginning in the 1930s, the Nazis had allied with the Muslim Brotherhood (MB), which would be an important part of fulfilling the secret Nazi plan for world control, perhaps coming to fulfillment today.

Hamas comes from the MB, and in Steven Emerson's *American Jihad: The Terrorists Living Among Us,* he listed Hamas as having groups and conventions in Oklahoma City. Relevant to the Oklahoma City bombing on April 19, 1995, Jim Crogan in "An Oklahoma Mystery: New hints of links between Timothy McVeigh and Middle Eastern terrorists" (*L.A. Weekly,* July 24–30, 2002) wrote that "an undated intelligence report by [director of the U.S. House of Representatives Task Force on Terrorism and Unconventional Warfare Yossef] Bodansky discusses alleged terrorist training inside the U.S. that included some 'Lily Whites.' . . . Bodansky states the training was ordered by Iran and conducted by Hamas operatives. . . . Bodansky's sources also report that at least two of the 1993 participants came from Oklahoma City."

Al-Qaeda also came from the MB, and its leader Osama bin Laden's father Mohammad bin Laden founded the Saudi Bin Laden Group in 1931. The group invested in the global satellite communications system Iridium (begun in November 1998), which would be used by the Pentagon for its communications. Seven months before the 9/11 attacks by al-Qaeda, National Security Agency (NSA) chief Gen. Mike Hayden on CBS's "60 Minutes" (February 13, 2001), revealed that "Osama bin Laden has at his disposal the wealth of a $3 trillion-a-year telecommunications industry that he can rely on.... He has better technology available to him than does the NSA."

Oklahoma City bomber Timothy McVeigh's alleged bombing partner, Terry Nichols, first met Ramzi Youssef (al-Qaeda 1993 World Trade Center bombing mastermind) in the Philippines on December 17, 1991. The FBI could have prevented the 1993 bombing, because the bomb designer asked his FBI contact to give him fake bomb-making material, but the contact didn't. The FBI also could have prevented the bombing of the Alfred P. Murrah Federal Building in Oklahoma City, but it prevented the Bureau of Alcohol, Tobacco, and Firearms (BATF) from its planned raid of Elohim City to arrest Andreas Strassmeir, described as the bombing "instigator."

Ramzi Youssef also planned Project Bojinka (where airplanes would be crashed into the World Trade Center, Pentagon, etc., like in the 9/11 attacks) and was in the Philippines with Abdul Hakim Murad, who told prison guards after the Oklahoma City bombing that Youssef's "Liberation Army" (a branch of al-Qaeda) was responsible for it. This is according to Paul Williams, consultant to the FBI, in *Al-Qaeda: Brotherhood of Terror* (2002). Williams also wrote that

> while making final preparations for Bojinka, the terrorists met with Terry Nichols several times in Cebu City, the Philippines. ... Some FBI officials now believe that Nichols ... obtained contact with Youssef through Muslim students at Southwest College [Southwestern Oklahoma State University] in Weatherford,

Oklahoma. The officials further believe that Youssef and Murad provided Nichols with training in making and handling bombs.... Several informants recently gave testimony that they met Nichols with Youssef in the Philippines and that the American was affectionately known there as "the Farmer."

Al-Qaeda's primary hiding place and training ground is in northwest Pakistan, whose head of intelligence services at the time of the 9/11 attacks, Gen. Mahmoud Ahmad, had $100,000 wired to 9/11 attack leader Mohammed Atta (an Egyptian and member of an engineering society associated with the MB) one month before the attacks. Atta had visited a flight school in Oklahoma, and in James Langston's "Iraqis Linked to Oklahoma Atrocity" (*Evening Standard*, London, October 21, 2002), one reads that "two of the Sept. 11th conspirators held a crucial meeting at a motel in Oklahoma City in August 2001. The motel's owner has since identified them as ringleader Mohammed Atta and Zacarias Moussaoui.... The motel is unremarkable—except for one thing. It is where a number of ... witnesses are sure they saw McVeigh drinking and perhaps plotting with his Iraqi friends."

This raises the possibility that the Oklahoma City bombing was an Iraqi attack, perhaps as part of the secret Nazi plan. Jon Dougherty in his WorldNetDaily article "Iraq link to OKC, Sept. 11 attacks?" (April 18, 2002) quotes Oklahoma City attorney John M. Johnston as saying his evidence "will show that the Republic of Iraq and Saddam Hussein were involved in funding and planning" the Oklahoma City bombing, and that "certain elements of the U.S. government must have known" about the "foreign involvement all along." One might remember at this point that according to UPI intelligence correspondent Richard Sale in "Exclusive: Saddam key in early CIA plot" (April 10, 2003), "Saddam's first contacts with U.S. officials date back to 1959, when he was part of a CIA-authorized six-man squad tasked with assassinating then Iraqi Prime Minister Gen. Abd al-Karim Qasim."

But why and how, you may ask, would this be part of the secret

Nazi plan? For the answer to this, you must remember that the Grand Mufti of Jerusalem, Hajj Amin al-Husseini was put on the Nazi payroll in 1938. And one of his confidantes was Saddam Hussein's uncle, Gen. Khairullah Tulfah, who became Saddam's mentor. According to Chuck Morse in *The Nazi Connection to Islamic Terrorism* (2003): "Clearly Saddam Hussein was tutored in the al-Husseini brand of Muslim Nazism by his uncle from an early age, and would become one of the most devout and effective practitioners of al-Husseini inspired Nazi pan-Arabism, as his career would attest."

In James Langston's article mentioned earlier, he indicates that the sketch of the Oklahoma City bombing suspect John Doe 2 is an almost perfect match for an Oklahoma City restaurant worker named Hussain al-Hussaini, who "has a tattoo on his upper left arm, indicating he was once a member of Saddam's elite Republican Guard." Furthermore, Micah Morrison in "The Iraq Connection" (*Wall Street Journal*, September 5, 2002) quotes Patrick Lang (former director of the Defense Intelligence Agency's Human Intelligence Collection Section) as having written that al-Hussaini was likely a member of Unit 999 of the Iraqi Military Intelligence Service, or Estikhabarat, headquartered at Salman Pak southeast of Baghdad, which "deals with clandestine operations at home and abroad."

And how does this connect with Oklahoma City bombing participants Timothy McVeigh and Terry Nichols? In the "Washington Whispers" section of *U.S. News and World Report* (October 29, 2001), one finds that "a few top Defense officials think Oklahoma City's bomber Timothy McVeigh was an Iraqi agent. The theory stems from a never-before-reported allegation that McVeigh had allegedly collected Iraqi telephone numbers. Why haven't we heard this before about the case of the executed McVeigh? Conspiracy theorists in the Pentagon think it's part of a cover-up." In addition, Kelly Patricia O'Meara in "Iraq Connections to U.S. Extremists" (*Insight Magazine*, December 3, 2001) wrote of the connection of Terry Nichols to elements of Iraqi intelligence.

I can't prove that the Oklahoma City bombing was part of the secret Nazi plan about which I have written, but it could be considered as being helpful in the fulfillment of the plan today. Most of the CIA's covert operations in the part of the world around Pakistan have been run through Pakistani intelligence (ISI). Of interest, and perhaps relevant to the secret Nazi plan, is that Germany was key in helping Pakistan get atomic weapons.

Between 200,000 and 300,000 second- and third-level Nazis went underground in Germany alone during WWII. They would be important in carrying out the secret Nazi plan for world control, as would thousands of high-level Nazis (e.g., SS members) who spread throughout the world.

The anniversary of the Oklahoma City bombing is on April 19, and the BBC show "Conspiracy Files" on March 4, 2007, contained speculation that the instigator of the bombing, Andreas Strassmeir, had ties to U.S. and German intelligence! Strassmeir had served in the German army in the area of intelligence (including disinformation). His father, Gunter, was a member of the Hitler Youth movement (Andreas' grandfather was a founding member of the Nazi Party), and chief-of-staff to German chancellor Helmut Kohl. In addition, Gunter Strassmeir was the father of the German reunification movement, and German reunification would also play an important part in carrying out the secret Nazi plan.

Vincent Petruskie helped Andreas Strassmeir get into the U.S., and Andreas referred to him as "a former CIA [OSS] guy my father had known" in Berlin during WWII. Petruskie had been an Air Force intelligence officer in Vietnam in the 1960s, and in the counterintelligence division in Washington, D.C., in the 1970s. He introduced Andreas to Black Mountain, North Carolina, attorney Kirk Lyons, whose grandfather was also a founding member of the Nazi Party.

After Andreas' discharge from the German army when he was twenty-seven, he flew to Washington, D.C., on April 7, 1989. This was about the same time Oklahoma City bomber Timothy McVeigh returned from Germany after his two-week "Change-Up Program" active-duty assignment with the German army. Also about this same time, McVeigh was assigned to Ft. Bragg in North Carolina, where double-agent Maj. Ali Mohamed (who worked with the CIA and the Egyptian Islamic Jihad, and trained members of al-Qaeda) was located. McVeigh told his sister in a letter that he was one of ten selected out of four hundred to be a member of a Special Forces secret team to "work for the government on the domestic, as well as international, fronts" including "helping the CIA fly drugs into the U.S. to fund many covert operations."

Investigator Bob Fletcher on Radio Liberty (March 20, 2012) related that CIA operative Gary Best had supplied the Contras in Nicaragua with timing instruments that blew up C4 explosives ("Iran-Contra" was a drug money-for-weapons deal) and was training mercenaries in Azerbaijan (which borders Iran) in the 1990s. Fletcher then revealed that just three months before the Oklahoma City bombing, Best bought a meat company only one and a half miles from the Alfred P. Murrah Federal Building in Oklahoma City, and ceremonially on the first anniversary of the bombing of that building filed company bankruptcy papers. Is this all just coincidental?

McVeigh also wrote to his sister, "We would be government-paid assassins!" He wrote this letter on October 20, 1993, about a week after he and Terry Nichols drove from Fayetteville, Arkansas, to Elohim City, Oklahoma, to meet Andreas Strassmeir.

Elohim City founder Robert Millar "was in regular contact with the [FBI] in the years before the bombing," according to June 31, 1997, testimony by senior FBI agent Peter Rickel. Another informant at Elohim City was Peter Langan, leader of the Aryan Republican Army and son of a retired U.S. Marine intelligence officer.

Attorney Kirk Lyons had introduced Strassmeir to Elohim City, and informant Carol Howe there sent to her BATF (Bureau of Alcohol, Tobacco and Firearms) officer Angela Finley seventy reports within which she indicated Strassmeir and others planned to blow up federal office buildings, including the Murrah Building in Oklahoma City. Two days after the bombing, Howe reminded the FBI that Strassmeir had "discussed assassinations, bombings and mass shootings" (this was in a November 29, 1994, BATF report by Howe's superior Angela Finley). Despite this, and despite the fact that the FBI interviewed over twenty thousand witnesses regarding the bombing, the FBI never interviewed Strassmeir before he left the U.S. in January 1996 (for months before he fled the U.S. he stayed with Kirk Lyons in Black Mountain, North Carolina).

Ambrose Evans-Pritchard in *The Secret Life of Bill Clinton: The Unreported Stories* (1997) judged that Strassmeir "was being protected by the Bureau [FBI]." Relevant to this, ABC's "20/20" segment on Carol Howe (February 5, 1997) was pulled at the last moment. When assistant producer retired Marine Lt. Col. Roger Charles saw it was never going to be aired, he protested, was fired, and told Evans-Pritchard that a message from this was "that this story would bring the country down, whatever that's supposed to mean."

In late spring of 1996, Evans-Pritchard had a series of conversations with Strassmeir, who was in Germany, in which the latter seemed to indicate that he worked for the American federal government but wouldn't say specifically for whom. When Evans-Pritchard asked Strassmeir why he didn't come forward and tell the whole story, the latter seemed to indicate he would be considered "a provocateur" who "talked and manipulated the others into" the bombing.

There's a new documentary regarding the Oklahoma City bombing called *A Noble Lie* which covers some of the information contained in this article, as well as evidence from seismic readings and witness testimony that the Murrah Building was severely damaged by more than a truck bomb of ammonium nitrate and fuel oil (ANFO bomb). A report using the Eglin Air Force Base Wright Laboratory test results regarding structural damage, etc., indicated the truck bomb explosion could not have been an ANFO bomb!

The report, "Case Study Relating Blast Effects Tests to the

Events of April 19, 1995, Alfred P. Murrah Building, Oklahoma City, Oklahoma," written by demolition expert John Culvertson, concluded: "Due to these conditions [relating to the inefficiency of air blasts in destroying reinforced concrete columns] it is impossible to ascribe the damage that occurred on April 19th, 1995, to a single truck bomb containing 4800 lbs. of ANFO [ammonium nitrate fuel oil mixture]. It must be concluded that the damage at the Murrah Federal Building is not the result of the truck bomb itself, but rather due to other factors such as locally placed charges within the building itself."

Many questions regarding the Oklahoma City bombing still have gone unanswered, including why would Strassmeir, if he was simply on an intelligence mission for Germany, become a bombing "provocateur"? Evans-Pritchard believes Strassmeir was a "shared asset," working for German intelligence and "on loan to the U.S. government," perhaps "the domestic services section of the CIA," which under usual procedures would pass Strassmeir's report "to the CIA's Directorate of Operations." Remember that in my book *The Power Elite and the Secret Nazi Plan*, I explain how Allen Dulles of the OSS and CIA, during and after WWII, worked with important Nazis such as Gen. Reinhard Gehlen, German military intelligence officer, and his Gehlen Organization. As I said before, I can't prove the Oklahoma City bombing was part of the secret Nazi plan which is being fulfilled today. However, the bombing along with the 9/11 attacks, economic crises, Middle Eastern and North African revolutions, etc., could be seen as helping in the plan's fulfillment.

A final question that perhaps will never be answered satisfactorily is whether Timothy McVeigh was really executed by the government if he was actually a government agent. The official story was that he was executed. However, if you look at the video clip, you will see and hear Susan Carlson of WLS in Chicago saying about the execution of McVeigh: "The shallow breathing continued . . . or what appeared to be shallow breathing . . . even after they pronounced him dead." While you are reflecting on this, remember that dead people don't breathe!

# A "Bold New World" and "Forces Too Powerful"

William Knoke was founder and president of the Harvard Capital Group, which advises "global corporations." And in his book *Bold New World: The Essential Road Map to the Twenty-First Century* (1996), Knoke projects that "in the twenty-first century, we will each retain our 'indigenous' cultures, our unique blend of tribal affiliations, . . . yet our passion for the large nation state, for which our ancestors fought with their blood, will dwindle to the same emotional consequences of county or province today. A new spirit of global citizenship will evolve in its place, and with it the ascendancy of global governance."

Knoke's vision is not new, as noted Fabian and historian Arnold Toynbee in a paper presented in early June 1931 remarked:

> A local state may lose its sovereignty without losing those familiar features which endear it to the local patriot—such features, I mean, as the local vernacular language and folklore and costume, and the local monuments of the historical past. . . . [But] if we are frank with ourselves, we shall admit that we are engaged on a deliberate and sustained and concentrated effort to impose limitations upon the sovereignty and the independence of the . . . sovereign independent States. . . . The dragon of local sovereignty can still use its teeth and claws when it is brought to bay. Nevertheless, I believe that the

monster is doomed to perish by our sword. The fifty or sixty local states of the world will no doubt survive as administrative conveniences. But sooner or later sovereignty will depart from them.

Toynbee was one of those individuals pursuing Cecil Rhodes' "scheme to take the government of the whole world!" His paper (quoted from above) was reprinted in the November 1931 edition of *International Affairs,* the journal of the Royal Institute of International Affairs, an outgrowth of the semi-secret Round Table Groups, formed between 1908 and 1913 to further Rhodes' plan for an elite to dominate the world. According to Bill Clinton's mentor at Georgetown University, Professor Carroll Quigley, in *Tragedy and Hope* (1966), the elite who formed the Round Table Groups "in 1919 founded the Royal Institute of International Affairs. . . . Similar Institutes of International Affairs were established in the chief British dominions and in the United States (where it is known as the Council on Foreign Relations)."

Whenever someone asks for evidence of a secret plan to undermine national sovereignty, the question invariably arises as to who are the elite behind the plan. In that regard, the Toynbee paper quoted above was read at the Fourth Annual Conference of Institutions for the Scientific Study of International Relations. Twelve countries were represented, along with delegates from four international organizations, and the conferences were initiated by the League of Nations Institute for Intellectual Cooperation. National coordinating committees were also formed, with one of their purposes being the execution of resolutions passed by the conferences. In the Toynbee paper quoted above, he stated (and note especially the word "we"):

> I will merely repeat that we are at present working, discreetly but with all our might, to wrest this mysterious political force called sovereignty out of the clutches of the local national states of the world. And all the time we are denying with our lips what we are doing with our hands, because to impugn the sovereignty of the

local nation states of the world is still a heresy for which a statesman or a publicist can be—perhaps not quite burnt at the stake, but certainly can be ostracized and discredited.

Concerning the preparation of an elite to dominate the world, Paul Mantoux wrote in the Foreword of *International Understanding: Agencies Educating for a New World* (1931) by John Eugene Harley: "How can a well-prepared elite be raised throughout the world to spread its influence over the masses, who can then support them in their turn? . . . Plainly the first step, in the case of each country, is to train an elite to think, feel, and act internationally." In order to do this in the U.S., though, our nationalistic Constitution would first have to be undermined. And in that regard, the next year (1932) William Kay Wallace's *Our Obsolete Constitution* was published. Wallace had accompanied President Wilson to Paris after World War I and was attached to the American Commission to Negotiate Peace. In his book, Wallace wrote:

> The age of individualism is past. . . . The Constitution is no longer adequate to meet the requirements of our age. . . . [The individual] must adopt the one best way or plan which has been scientifically determined by experts. . . . The absurdity of such doctrines as those of national rights and a social contract has long been recognized. . . . As we have gone beyond the stage of believing in an avenging God, so we are coming to realize that ideas of political sovereignty are borrowings from ignorant notions about the source of power in the state. . . . Sovereignty in its narrow territorial aspects must be abandoned. . . . We must be prepared to integrate Scientific Capitalism with the principle of Scientific Socialism. . . . It is admitted on all sides that national directive control of industry . . . must be undertaken in the immediate future. . . . The state will control the means of production. . . .

The same year (1932), Rhodes scholar Clyde Eagleton's *International*

*Government* was published, and in the Preface of the 1948 revised edition, he stated: "I am . . . concerned with . . . the slowly evolving constitutional law and organization of the community of nations developing toward international, or world, government." In the text of the book, he noted that "the following arguments have been offered in favor of regionalism: (1) Development should be attempted gradually, rather than in one jump toward world government. Such a world system could be better built upon the solid foundation of regional systems."

Concerning the pursuit of world government via regionalism, Graeme Howard in *America and a New World Order* (1940) argued regarding "the framework for support of the new world order" that "promising both a more ethical and a more realistic solution is the formation of regional economic entities. . . . Cooperative regionalism [will] bring about a better world order through internationally balanced economic and political regional blocs." Similarly, M. J. Bonn in *The Annals of American Academy of Political and Social Science* (July 1941) wrote that "national planning means deliberate international anarchy. . . . But we are not yet going to have a world state. . . . The formation of regional federations by hitherto autonomous groups of countries is much easier. . . . With every move a step toward a new world order is taken." And the next year, in *Post-War Worlds*, P. E. Corbett (also a member of the group furthering Rhodes' plan) wrote: "A world association binding together and coordinating regional groupings of states may evolve toward one universal federal government, as in the past loose confederations have grown into federal unions. . . . World government is the ultimate aim, but there is more chance of attaining it by gradual development."

The same year (1942), the Federal Council of Churches convened a "Commission to Study the Basis of a Just and Durable Peace" (in June 1996, Bishop William Swing convened an interfaith forum, "United Religions," as a prelude to Mikhail Gorbachev's second State of the World Forum in October 1996). The 1942 commission published a series of lectures titled *A Basis for the Peace to Come*, and in John Foster Dulles' lecture, "Toward World Order," he declared:

> We have found that regional integration . . . is not alone adequate. . . . We must find a system of government which can exercise jurisdiction which is worldwide. . . . Let us first consider the solution of 'world government.' . . . It involves an organization dedicated to the general welfare—the peace and order of mankind—and the assuming of an allegiance to this goal superior to that of any national allegiance. . . . By these . . . initial steps we will have begun that dilution of sovereignty which all enlightened thinkers agree to be indispensable.

Just think, President Eisenhower would choose this man to be his secretary of state, even though Dulles had these views regarding our national sovereignty.

In September 1942 *Free World* "Round Table No. 10" (remember Cecil Rhodes and the Round Table Groups), titled "The Coming World Order." In addition to Frank Aydelotte (American secretary to the Rhodes Trustees), participants included Clyde Eagleton (mentioned above) and William Allan Neilson, who was presiding. In the Round Table discussion, Neilson stated: "The question as to whether humanity is ready for world order, whether there are certain changes in public opinion that must be brought about first and what forces must be put to work for it, really follows very closely from this question of whether we should plan for it now while we are still at war."

Remember, this is in 1942, long before the end of the Second World War. Eagleton in the discussion proposed:

> What I had in mind was my hope that the United Nations, when they are victorious after this war, and assuming that they will be, would simply take over and run the world for a period of time, for a transitional period, and that they would compel other states to

obey and that they would ultimately change this United Nations system to a permanent world order in which every state must be a member and must submit to the regulations laid down by the international government.... But probably it will not be necessary to use coercion against them, because in such a world order, they would practically be compelled to fit in.

Neilson then interjected, "The economic pressure would be enough." One might remember this statement in terms of GATT and the World Trade Organization. *Free World* later published "Round Table No. 11" titled "Prospects for 1942" with one of the "Essential Findings" given as the following: "The creation of the machinery of a world government in which the present United Nations will serve as a nucleus is a necessary task of the present in order to prepare in time the foundation for a future world order."

And in the November 1942 *Free World*, T. V. Soong (minister for foreign affairs of the Chinese Republic) wrote "The Coming International Order," in which he declared:

> The new world order, like the Chinese Republic, and all like human institutions, will never be realized until we start it. And we shall never be more ready for starting it than now.... We are seeing more clearly than ever before ... the crying necessity for a new world order.... We must give to our young men, who are called on to sacrifice, a flaming mission of a new world order, and we must begin to make that mission come true now.

In 1946, the World Movement for World Federal Government was formed, and in 1947 the movement's philosophy was expressed in its Montreaux declaration. According to Alfred Lilienthal in *Which Way to World Government?* (Foreign Policy Association "Headline Series" number 83, Sept.–Oct. 1950), "At Montreaux the formation of regional federations, in so far as they did not become an end in themselves, was favorably regarded as a step toward the effective functioning of world government." In September 1946, Winston Churchill advocated a European Union and on May 13, 1947, stated: "Unless some effective world supergovernment, for the purposes of preventing war, can be set up and begin to reign, the prospects for peace and human progress are dark and doubtful. . . . But let there be no mistake upon one point. Without a United Europe there is no prospect of world government. It is the urgent and indispensable step toward the realization of that goal."

In that same year (1947), Cord Meyer, Jr. (who was a member of Scroll & Key at Yale University, as was Dean Acheson) became the first president of United World Federalists, and in *Peace or Anarchy?* (1947), he advocated "the transformation of the U.N. into a limited world government," and further stated:

> The U.N. must be given the constitutional authority to maintain security through laws which call for obedience from the individual inhabitants of the world as their first duty and which no national government can override. . . . They will not have the right to appeal to their national governments for protection because in its limited sphere the world law will be supreme. . . . Disarmament must be enforced by law and the possession of war-making power by national governments prohibited. They can be allowed to retain only the weapons needed for the maintenance of domestic order. . . . Similarly a limit must be set on the number of troops that any government can be allowed to retain. The abolition of mass armies is as essential as the outlawry of heavy armament. . . . The U.N. must have its own police and military forces to uphold its laws. A revised Charter must empower the U.N. to raise, train and support under its own command individuals owing exclusive allegiance to it. . . . The amended Charter should deny the right to secede. If it is to guarantee protection, the U.N. cannot allow the member nations the right to withdraw when they see fit. . . . So long as the present

sovereign state system exists, each government will continue to distort the education of its youth with nationalistic propaganda.

The tribal religion of nationalism is kept alive by the continuous menace of war. . . . Many of these proposals may appear unpatriotic or even treasonous to those who identify patriotism with the worship of American military power. . . . The tribal nationalists continue to believe that the support of a heavily armed and sovereign United States is the first duty of a citizen. . . . The final stage in the transference of power to the U.N. will be completed when the outlawed armaments have been removed from all national arsenals and national armies have been reduced to the size required for internal policing.

In March of the next year (1948), Meyer told the *New York Herald Tribune Forum*: "It is not a question of whether some kind of world government will be established in the next ten years. Within a decade the world will be organized as one political unit. It is only a question as to what kind of world government will be established, and how." Meyer will be a member of the Council on Foreign Relations and will work for the CIA from 1951 to 1977.

William Knoke in his book *Bold New World* mentioned earlier sees clearly the trend today toward world government via regional arrangements, as he comments that

Historians looking back on us today will view regional blocs as mere stepping-stones toward the world as a trading bloc, perhaps one political unit. . . . It will only be a matter of time before these blocs in turn, merge into a whole. . . . As each bloc forms, regional trade heightens and the need for a common currency, uniform product labeling, and commercial regulation rises. In each case, we are experimenting with new ways to link countries, to yield sovereignty in exchange for something more than what is lost.

It was evident even before the end of the Second World War that if a world government were to succeed, there would have to be some sort of enforcement mechanism. In the Chinese ambassador to the United States Hu Shih's lecture in *A Basis for the Peace to Come*, he pronounced: "The new world order which we want to see set up . . . must be a 'League to Enforce Peace.' . . . This new world order must command a sufficient amount of organized force to support its law and judgment."

The secretary-general of the United Nations, U Thant, would see the U.N. in the role of "enforcer," as in a May 6, 1962, address at Uppsala University in Sweden, he talked about "the myth of the absolute sovereign state," stating that

> If the United Nations is to grow into a really effective instrument for maintaining the rule of law, the first step must be the willingness of Member states to give up the concept of the absolute sovereign state. . . . In the community of nations, it is increasingly important to restrict the sovereignty of states, even in a small way to start with. This restriction may involve . . . the reduction of armed forces and the undertaking to submit disputes to the arbitration of an international judiciary. . . . The United Nations . . . must have the right, the power, and the means to keep the peace.

(See volume VI of the *Public Papers of the Secretaries-General of the United Nations*, made possible by a grant from the Ford Foundation, whose earlier president, H. Rowan Gaither, told Congressional Committee Research director Norman Dodd that the foundation was operating under directives from the White House "to the effect that we should make every effort to so alter life in the United States as to make possible a comfortable merger with the Soviet Union.")

In a later address to the World Association of World Federalists on August 23, 1970, in Ottawa, U Thant indicated "there is no aspect of world affairs and national affairs that does not require the attention of world citizens as they work steadfastly to usher in the new world order." And the next year (1971), U Thant became one of the founders of Planetary Citizens, along with Norman Cousins who would be president of the World Federalist Association. President Barack Obama has referred to himself as a "citizen of the world."

Cousins had earlier written in *Modern Man Is Obsolete* (1945):

> The greatest obsolescence of all in the Atomic Age is national sovereignty. . . . We even debate the question of "surrendering" some of our sovereignty—as though there is still something to surrender. There is nothing left to surrender. There is only something to gain. . . . A common world sovereignty would mean that no state could act unilaterally in its foreign affairs. . . . It would mean that no state could withdraw from the central authority as a method of achieving its aims. . . . There is no need to talk of the difficulties in the way of world government. There is need only to ask whether we can afford to do without it.

And if the U.N. were to become a *de facto* world government, how might it govern and who might be the model for its leadership? In a message to a UNESCO symposium in Finland in 1970, U Thant noted that "Lenin was a man with a mind of great clarity and incisiveness, and his ideas have had a profound influence on the course of contemporary history. . . . [Lenin's] ideals of peace and peaceful coexistence among states . . . are in line with the aims of the U.N. Charter." (See"Lenin Aims Like U.N.'s, Thant Says," *Los Angeles Times*, April 7, 1970.)

U Thant was not the only notable to see the "benefits" of the communist model for world government, as former U.S. Supreme Court Justice William O. Douglas in *Towards a Global Federalism* (1968) wrote that

> when the anatomy of that system [communism] is exposed, say at the level of medicare, scientific research and development,

athletics and the arts, technical training, nursery schools, outer space, the regime obviously reflect much that is good from the view point of all humanity.... "Building bridges" with Communist nations is the prime necessity of the day.... We have moved from free enterprise to a *sui generis* form of socialism. The trend toward the collective society will continue.... The Western and the Soviet regimes may yet evolve into comparable economic systems.... The new [global] federalism would deal with conflicts between nations just as our own Supreme Court deals with conflicts between sovereign states.

This is the type of synthesis I have mentioned many times as the goal of the PE. And Justice Douglas' 1968 assessment that we had already moved toward a form of socialism has been furthered by President Obama.

Unlike Lenin's acceptance of violent means to accomplish his ends, the movement today toward a world socialist government, synthesizing Western capitalism and Eastern communism, is more sophisticated and psychological in its approach. In that regard, Soviet defector Golitsyn in *The Perestroika Deception* (1995) spelled out how Mikhail Gorbachev had been tricking the West, as Gorbachev and his wife Raisa were the disciples of the late Sardinian communist Antonio Gramsci, "the Marxist proponent of a policy of active social demoralization" to undermine a country by subverting the culture through a variety of means. Though Gorbachev was responsible for numerous atrocities, he was treated royally when he toured the U.S., even having the use of Steve Forbes' (presidential candidate at the time) family airplanes.

Relevant to societal change and the movement toward a world socialist government, Knoke in his book projected that the socialist-dominated European Union "is showing us the next step.... What happens in Europe will very much be the model for world consolidation in the twenty-first century, not just economically, but politically and socially as well." But how would American society be changed to accept this "Grand Design"?

In Raymond Fosdick's memorial volume on Rockefeller's General Education Board, he described the Board as part of Rockefeller's effort toward "this goal of social control." And in 1945, Rockefeller Foundation medical director Alan Gregg was touring various institutions that had been involved in war medicine to see if any group would commit to undertake the kind of social psychiatry that had been developed by the Army during wartime (e.g., cultural psychiatry for the analysis of the enemy mentality), and see if it could be relevant for the civilian society.

This led to a Rockefeller grant that resulted in the birth of the Tavistock Institute of Human Relations in London in 1947. Tavistock would join with Kurt Lewin's Research Center for Group Dynamics at the University of Michigan the next year to begin publication of the international journal *Human Relations,* relating theory to practice. In that same year (1947), the Research Center for Group Dynamics along with a division of the National Education Association (NEA) founded the National Training Laboratories (NTL), which in 1962 published *Issues in* [Human Relations] *Training*. In this book is described "unfreezing, changing and refreezing" attitudes, and how the NTL has moved toward "sensitivity training" which is characterized as "thought reform or brainwashing." Some years later (1977) Tavistock senior staff member Fred Emery's *Futures We Are In* was published, in which was related Emery's theory of "social turbulence," which indicates that faced with a series of crises, many individuals will attempt to reduce the tension by adaptation and eventually psychological retreat, which can lead to social disintegration. Tavistock and the NTL have been especially interested in "human resource management" and "group behavior."

At this point, it is important to look a little more closely at who has been psychologically manipulating the American people as well as many others in the rest of the world. In that regard, Christopher

Simpson in *Science of Coercion: Communication Research and Psychological Warfare 1945–1960* (Oxford University Press, 1994) wrote:

> I first discuss U.S. psychological warfare prior to 1945, stressing the early work of noted communication theorists Harold Lasswell and Walter Lippmann and the pioneer studies underwritten by the Rockefeller Foundation.... Lasswell and Lippmann advocated... a particular social order in the United States and the world in which forceful elites necessarily ruled in the interests of their vision of the greater good. U.S.-style consumer democracy was simply a relatively benign system for engineering mass consent for the elite's authority.... Harold Lasswell had the ear of [Rockefeller] Foundation administrator John Marshall.... The elite of U.S. society ("those who have money to support research," as Lasswell bluntly put it) should systematically manipulate mass sentiment.

A key agent of such elite was John J. McCloy, assistant secretary of war during World War II, who established a highly secret psychology branch within the War Department General Staff G-2 (Intelligence) organization (McCloy would go on to become head of the World Bank, on the board of the Rockefeller Foundation, chairman of the Ford Foundation, and chairman of the Council on Foreign Relations for many years). Other elite such as William Paley (CBS), C. D. Jackson (Time/Life) and W. Phillips Davison (RAND) were prominent staff members of the U.S. Army's psychological warfare division during the Second World War. Two other centers of psychological warfare at that time were the Office of War Information (OWI) headed by Rhodes scholar Elmer Davis, and Samuel Stouffer's research branch of the U.S. Army's Division of Morale.

After the war, Stouffer (Harvard University) became a member of the interservice Committee on Human Resources established by the Department of Defense in 1947. John Clauson, who was a veteran of Stouffer's research branch, wrote in "Research on the American

Soldier As a Career Contingency" (*Social Psychology Quarterly*, vol. 47, no. 2, 1984):

> Perhaps most intriguing was the number of our members who became foundation executives. Charles Dollard became president of Carnegie Corporation. Donald Young shifted from the presidency of SSRC (Social Science Research Council) to that of Russell Sage. . . . Leland DeVinney went from Harvard to the Rockefeller Foundation. William McPeak . . . helped to set up the Ford Foundation and became its vice president. W. Parker Mauldin became vice president of the Population Council. The late Lyle Spencer (of Science Research Associates) . . . endowed a foundation that currently supports a substantial body of social science research.

Dollard (president of the Carnegie Corporation 1948–1954) and Young (SSRC) urged Stuart Chase (with the League for Industrial Democracy, formerly titled The Intercollegiate Socialist Society) to write *The Proper Study of Mankind*. The book was initially financed by Carnegie Corporation, was characterized as a project of the SSRC, and was published in by Harper and Brothers in 1948. In the book, one reads:

> Theoretically a society could be completely made over in something like fifteen years, the time it takes to inculcate a new culture into a rising crop of youngsters. . . . Prepare now for a surprising universe: Individual talent is too sporadic and unpredictable to be allowed any important part in the organization of society. Social systems which endure are built on the average person who can be trained to occupy any position adequately if not brilliantly.

Does this not call to mind Pavlov's conditioning of dogs in the past and outcome-based or school-to-work education today?

And how society would be "made over" by Chase can be seen in his earlier book, *A New Deal* (Chase originated this term and would be a member of FDR's "Kitchen Cabinet"), in 1932 in which he proclaimed:

> I am not seriously alarmed by the sufferings of the creditor class, the troubles which the church is bound to encounter, the restrictions on certain kinds of freedom which must result, nor even by the bloodshed of the transition period. A better economic order is worth a little bloodshed. . . . Revolution can give what no other road promises to give so directly and forcibly—a new religion. . . . It will be materialistic. . . . We need a new religion. . . . Red revolution is a creed, dramatic, idealistic and, in the long run, constructive. . . . A nation [Russia] of 160 million people . . . has adopted this religion. . . . Groups are actually beginning to form. As yet they are scattered and amorphous; here a body of engineers, there a body of economic planners. Watch them. They will bear watching. If occasion arises, join them. They are part of what H. G. Wells has called the Open Conspiracy. Why should Russians have all the fun remaking the world?

Chase would be a consultant to UNESCO in 1949.

Dollard was not only president of the Carnegie Corporation (and a trustee of RAND), but he was also chairman of the human relations panel of the Defense Department's Committee on Human Resources (paid panel consultants included Lasswell and the Carnegie Corporation's John Gardner, who would become secretary of HEW under President Johnson). In Christopher Simpson's book mentioned above, the author states that "it was the Carnegie executives who controlled the purse strings of the funds on which Stouffer relied."

Like John Clauson's statement earlier in this chapter, former OWI overseas director Edward Barrett (head of the U.S. government's overt psychological warfare program 1950–1952, and later dean of the Columbia University Graduate School of Journalism) in *Truth Is Our Weapon* (1953) wrote:

> Among OWI alumni are the publishers of *Time, Look, Fortune,* and several dailies; editors of such magazines as *Holiday, Coronet, Parade,* and the *Saturday Review,* editors of the *Denver Post, New Orleans Times-Picayune,* and others; the heads of Viking Press, Harper & Brothers, and Farrar, Straus and Young . . . the board chairman of CBS and a dozen key network executives . . . the editor of *Reader's Digest* international editions. . . .

Christopher Simpson in *Science of Coercion* reveals that

> U.S. psychological warfare programs between 1945 and 1960 provide a case study of how the priorities and values of powerful social groups can be transformed into the "received knowledge" of the scientific community and, to a certain extent, of society as a whole . . . the engineering of consent of targeted populations at home and abroad. . . . Various leaders in the social sciences engaged one another in tacit alliances to promote their particular interpretations of society. . . . They regarded mass communication as a tool for social management and as a weapon in social conflict. . . . Key academic journals of the day . . . concentrated on how modern technology could be used by elites to manage social change, extract political concessions, or win purchasing decisions from targeted audiences. . . . This orientation reduced the extraordinarily complex, inherently communal process of communication to simple models based on the dynamics of transmission of persuasive—and, in the final analysis, coercive—messages.

Since that time, commercial advertisers have increasingly used psychological techniques of persuasion upon the American public, and Simpson notes:

> From the advertisers' point of view, the simple sale of products and services is not enough. Their commercial success in a mass market depends to an important degree on their ability to substitute their values and worldview for those previously held by their audience.
> ... Terms like "Pepsi Generation," "Heartbeat of America," and "I Love What You Do for Me" have always been more than simple advertisement slogans. They have been successful from the advertisers' point of view only to the extent they have defined a way of life.

Concerning the subject of education, as American education continued to decline through the 1970s and 1980s, corporations became increasingly concerned that they would not have enough skilled workers to compete in what they saw as the new "global economy." Management of "human resources" or "human capital" to compete in such an economy became of prime importance to industry.

On May 8, 1996, A. D., a co-worker of Dr. Shirley McCune at the federally-funded Mid-Continent Regional Educational Laboratory (McREL) told me that McCune (who left McREL around 1994) had referred to work done at the Research Center for Group Dynamics, founded in 1946 by Kurt Lewin. The co-worker said he believed that McCune had known Lewin and had done work for the National Training Laboratories (NTL). Prior to coming to McREL, McCune had been a director of the tax-funded Education Commission of the States (ECS) and had been with the (John) Naisbitt (author of *Megatrends*) Group. After coming to McREL, McCune authored a 63–page working paper in 1983 for the Kansas State Department of Education titled "Framing a Future for Education."

The working paper was largely based upon the views expressed in *Megatrends,* and McCune stated: "Schools must become more effective and more efficient in providing society with human resources which are essential for our national well-being." She continued to say that students will be expected to develop "ability to work in groups, use skills in critical thinking, problem solving . . . synthesizing, decision making and communication—key factors for successful participation in the work force." Students would be the products or "human capital" for society's economic system, and there would be "lifelong learning" with an increase in adult education and retraining. McCune went on to say, "The future of all institutions and our total society rests on our ability to develop human capital or to 'grow better people.'"

Under "Probable Directions for Restructuring Education," she listed among the "Goals of Education" in "An Information Society" the following: "Global education, small group skills, computer as learning tool in all programs, and career/vocational education as integral part of educational community experience." Also under "Probable Directions" in "An Information Society," she included "School-based management, managed change, economic development [forming human capital], expanded support for total population services, business as participant and learning resource, school as community center for various ages and services, lifelong learning oriented."

On November 2, 1989, McCune spoke at the Kansas Governor's Conference on Education, stating that

> The Governors began to understand the very close relationship between economic development and human capital. . . . What we're into is the total restructuring of the society. . . . What I'm not sure that we have begun to comprehend or to act on sufficiently is the incredible amount of . . . human resource development restructuring. . . . In this particular changed society, there are only two things that really matter . . . and secondly to produce human capital. . . . The great majority of businessmen today understand the critical importance of human resource development. . . . More and more the school is the cob or the center of all human resource development services. . . . We have to have adults who can be leaders, leaders who can, in fact, have visions of where we can go in the future. . . . We have to prepare students for the range of knowledge

and skills they'll need . . . with group and organizational skills . . . conflict resolution skills. . . . We're going to have to provide them with career development skills. . . . One of the developments that's going on in more and more communities in this nation . . . [is] an educator whose job is to work with the social welfare community and put together a total network of human resource development activities in that community where we can actually provide for all of the needs of the children and of the adults in that community. . . . The earlier we intervene into the lives of people, the cheaper it is.

What Dr. Shirley McCune was saying is a fulfillment of what Arthur Calhoun wrote in the third volume of his 1919 book, *A Social History of the American Family*, in which he proclaimed:

The modern individual is a world citizen, served by the world, and home interests can no longer be supreme. . . . As familism weakens, society has to assume a larger parenthood. The school begins to assume responsibility for the functions thrust upon it. . . . The kindergarten grows downward toward the cradle and there arises talk of neighborhood nurseries. . . . Social centers replace the old time home chimney. . . . The child passes more and more into the custody of community experts. . . . It seems clear that at least in its early stages, socialism will mean an increased amount of social control. . . . We may expect in the socialist commonwealth a system of public educational agencies that will begin with the nursery and follow the individual through life. . . . Those persons that experience alarm at the thought of intrinsic changes in family institutions should remember that in the light of social evolution, nothing is right or valuable in itself.

At about the same time, McCune delivered the main speech at an Aurora, Colorado, "in-service" teachers session, and according to a teacher there, McCune proclaimed:

> Radical change is necessary now; you cannot escape it. . . . Strategies and behaviors must be changed because the dawning of this new age is far more significant than the transformation of the national and world economics which is taking place. . . . The [new] Information Society will touch every aspect of our lives. It will shape a new social character or person who views the world in very different ways. . . . The schools will become the training institutions whose function it is to affect all other sectors of society—economic, social, and political.

And what kind of radically changed, restructured New Age society and education did Dr. McCune have in mind? In *The Light Shall Set You Free* (1996), she talked about a "point of light," and stated:

> Only the souls who are ready to receive the new curriculum will elect to raise their vibrations to match those required to enter the New Age. . . . Did you know that the animals' souls are the souls of our future children? . . . We are entering the Age of Aquarius. . . . The goal for all of humanity who will enter the new millennium is to become androgynous. . . . Educational systems, businesses, political structures and governments all built on self-serving principals, for example, are crumbling, only to be reborn through tremendous pain into higher forms.

At about the same time Dr. McCune co-authored this book she was a research assistant in School-to-Work at Arizona State University, and then she became an administrative assistant to the superintendent of public instruction for the State of Washington.

Much of the information in her book is alleged to have been channeled through the authors by "Ascended Masters," including one called "El Morya, Master." And this is where there is an international connection.

For decades, the U.S. has poured millions of U.S. tax dollars into the U.N., and for decades while secretary-generals came and went, Robert Muller remained an assistant secretary-general. While at the U.N., he began the Robert Muller School in Arlington, Texas, and his schools are in over twenty-five nations and are members of the UNESCO Associated Schools Project. A description of Muller's school from its own document states that: "The underlying philosophy upon which the Robert Muller School is based will be found in the teachings set forth in the books of Alice A. Bailey by the . . . teachings of M. Morya. . . ." This is the "El Morya, Master" mentioned in Dr. McCune's book, and Alice Bailey was the leading occultist of the first half of the twentieth century. Bailey wrote often about a coming "new world order" and "points of light" connected to service. Her first works were published by Lucifer Publishing Company, which became Lucis Trust, now located at 120 Wall Street in New York City.

That Dr. McCune is a New Age proponent who on November 2, 1989, had used the term "human resource development" more than once is perhaps significant in that earlier in that year, New Age networking senator Claiborne Pell had introduced Senate Joint Resolution 135, the "National Commission on Human Resource Development Act," co-sponsored by senators Al Gore and Nancy Kassebaum. The resolution was to establish the Center for Human Resource Development and spoke of the "normal aspiration of all citizens to more fully achieve their potential in body, mind and spirit. . . . [And] there is a role for government to assist in research and education on techniques that promote the . . . fuller realization of human potential." Testifying for the measure was Dr. Herbert Benson of Harvard Medical School, who explained the "relaxation response" as experienced by those who practice Zen, yoga and transcendental meditation. The resolution probably would have passed the Senate except that Senator Dan Coates put a "hold" on it and it died.

Before continuing with the subject of education, I will digress briefly to describe the effect of the New Age upon the presidency. Not only did *Newsweek* refer to Bill Clinton as the first "New Age

President," but the "Renaissance Weekend" he had attended for years was referred to by *The New York Times* as a "New Age Retreat." Then, in a front-page article in *The Washington Post* (June 23, 1996), Bob Woodward wrote that Hillary Clinton "seemed jerked around by the muddled role of first lady, as she swung between New Age feminist and national housewife." Woodward was excerpting from his new book, *The Choice*, and recounted that at Camp David on the weekend of December 30, 1994, Bill and Hillary Clinton invited people to dissect the first two years of his presidency and search for a way back from the Democrats' congressional defeat in November of that year. Woodward related that Jean Houston "played a significant role over the weekend and the year that followed. . . . Hillary and Houston clicked, especially during a discussion of how to use the office [of the presidency] for the betterment of society."

Houston is a New Age researcher in psychic experiences and altered consciousness, who has visited and worked in thirty-six countries under the auspices of UNESCO, and who spoke on "The Rise of the New Right" at the National Education Association convention in 1979. She has been a director of the syncretistic Temple of Understanding, and has spoken to the National Catholic Educational Association annual convention several times. On March 14, 1989, she spoke on "Whole System Transition: The Birth of the Planetary Society" to the Association for Supervision and Curriculum Development (ASCD) annual conference (the day after New Age former U.N. assistant secretary-general Robert Muller spoke to the ASCD on "Educating the Global Citizen: Illuminating the Issues," which was the conference theme). Houston along with John Naisbitt (remember Shirley McCune's connection to him, and McCune also participated in the 1989 ASCD conference) and Elsa Porter (President Jimmy Carter's assistant secretary of commerce) founded The Possible Society, which in 1985 sponsored a seminar in Denver re-creating *The Wonderful Wizard of Oz,* with Houston employing trances, etc., and saying "You are simply God in hiding. You must achieve your potential Godhood." This same year *Newsweek* published "The Megatrends Man" (September 23, 1985) about John Naisbitt, and in the article referred to "the crowd of 200 or so mostly New Age enthusiasts. . . . Senator Albert Gore of Tennessee, a friend of the Naisbitts and one of the invited speakers, got into the swing of things by submitting that it was time to 're-think the nation-state system.'" (In Gore's book *Earth in the Balance*, he says: "Nature in its fullest is God.") In Jennifer Donovan's article "Creating Mythos of the Modern World" (*San Francisco Chronicle*, March 19, 1985) about Jean Houston, Donovan wrote that Houston was "a showman and shaman . . . calling what she does 'priestcraft.'"

In Bob Woodward's *Washington Post* article mentioned above, he also wrote: "Houston and her work were controversial because she believed in spirits and other worlds, put people into trances and used hypnosis, and because in the 1960s she had conducted experiments with LSD. . . . [Houston] conducted extensive dialogues with Athena [pagan Greek deity] on her computer." Woodward then indicated that while Houston did not use any of these aforementioned techniques on Bill and Hillary Clinton, Houston at the White House in April 1995 did put Hillary through a visualization exercise, asking Hillary to shut her eyes and visualize meeting Eleanor Roosevelt. Woodward wrote, "Houston regarded it as a classic technique, practiced by Machiavelli, who used to talk to ancient men." Hillary was then asked by Houston to play the part of and speak as Mrs. Roosevelt, and then Houston asked Hillary to visualize speaking to Mahatma Gandhi. Woodward revealed that in October and November 1995, "Houston virtually moved into the White House residence for several days at a time to help" with Hillary's book *It Takes a Village*. And Woodward concluded the article by writing "Houston wondered what might happen if her role as advisor and friend to the first couple became public. 'If I ever get caught,' Houston asked Hillary, 'what should I say?' 'Just tell the truth,' Hillary replied, 'Just tell them you're my friend.'"

According to the *Encyclopedia of Occultism & Parapsychology*,

Houston and her sexologist husband, Robert Masters, developed something known as "the Witches' Cradle." In March 1968, the NTL Institute (mentioned earlier in this chapter), presented a week-long seminar by Jean Houston and her staff titled "The Myth and Mystery of Isis and Osiris: A Journey of Transformation." And in 1995, Houston authored *The Passion of Isis and Osiris: A Union of Two Souls*. Given that Bob Woodward felt it important to show Hillary's connection to Houston and Houston's "dialogues with Athena," one must wonder why the press did not explore Bob Dole's being a Shriner "noble" of Isis Temple (Isis was a pagan Egyptian deity) for some forty years in Salina, Kansas. And given that Athena is important to Jean Houston, it is relevant that *The Encyclopedia of Mythology* indicates Athena "played a predominant role in the construction of the Trojan Horse, which she was said to have dreamed up." Could it be that Jean Houston introduced the "Trojan Horse" of New Age spirituality into the White House and society at large to change the nation's consciousness away from Judeo-Christian moral absolutes? Remember, New Ager Dr. Shirley McCune said: "What we're into is the total restructuring of society."

Not only is the "Trojan Horse" a useful device for gradualist change agents to alter people's spiritual values, but their political-economic values, too. In *The Autobiography of James T. Shotwell* (1961), this director of the Carnegie Endowment for International Peace described his plan developed in the early 1930s for lessening international trade barriers. Shotwell had helped plan the League of Nations and the U.N., as well as inspire the founding of the International Labor Organization. And in his autobiography, he said:

> The main idea was simple—nations which raised the wages and standard of living in the production of goods should have favored tariff treatment in the country to which they were exported. The plan was directed against the argument for high tariffs because of low wage costs in other countries. . . . Neither Mr. [Cordell] Hull

[FDR's secretary of state) nor his economic assistants liked the scheme, because of its lack of fundamental free trade principle. I said it was the Trojan Horse to get inside the protectionist walls.

Shotwell's strategy reached its fulfillment with the enactment of GATT and the World Trade Organization (WTO) as part of the globalist elite's plan to have a global economy as a prelude to a global civilization. On NBC's "Today Show" (June 26, 1996), Jean Houston said, "We're moving towards a Planetary Civilization," and the New Age movement fits well with the globalist elite's plan also to use educational reform (transformation) to help facilitate their desired world socialist government.

That a world socialist government is the goal of the PE can be seen in PE agent and world federalist Mortimer Adler's *Haves Without Have-Nots* (1991) in which he asserted that the U.S., NATO, the Soviet Union, etc. will be replaced by the USDR (Union of Socialist Democratic Republics). Political and economic homogeneity will occur in "a new First World order in the next century" (twenty-first century), as there will be a redistribution of wealth from the "have" to the "have-not" nations (concept supported by the Earth Charter and President Barack Obama). Adler professed that "this can be done only by the regulation of a world economy by a world government." All participating nations must be "socialist," and surrender "every vestige of national sovereignty in dealing with one another." World government would preclude nations' "foreign policies, military installations and personnel, and immigration barriers." Because there has been a resurgent emotional attachment to nationalism today, Adler believed that it may be overcome only by causing people to have an "emotionally felt" reaction to "the threat of irreversible damage to the environment . . . to prevent the destruction of the biosphere."

The New Age often emphasizes Eastern mysticism. Zen Buddhism along with Confucianism, Shintoism, and other Eastern religions emphasize loyalty to one's group and/or one's relationship to "nature." Christianity, however, emphasizes each individual's personal relationship with Jesus and each person's need for salvation by Christ. Traditional American education emphasizes individual initiative, but educational reformers today are pushing outcome-based education (OBE) which emphasizes "the group" (e.g., cooperative learning). Similarly, traditional American values emphasize individual responsibility, but socialism emphasizes the government's (through the group's) responsibility (e.g., the welfare state).

Regarding education, some years ago the Carnegie Corporation began to fund initiatives to transform American education to prepare a skilled workforce (along with negotiating the Soviet-American Exchange Agreement in late 1985). This included OBE (group-oriented) school-to-work (STW) initiatives, which would fit neatly into the socialist world to come. Then in 1992, the National Center (formerly Carnegie Forum) on Education and the Economy (NCEE) produced a Human Resources Development Plan that seemed quite similar in a number of ways to what Dr. Shirley McCune had earlier proposed. The NCEE plan would integrate education into a national (cradle-to-grave) outcome-based and performance-based system of human resources development, including apprenticeships somewhat like those in Germany.

National borders would be meaningless in the socialist world to come, as Robert Reich (who would become President Clinton's secretary of labor) in *The Work of Nations* (1991) stated that in the coming century, "There will be no national products or technologies, no national corporations, no national industries. There will no longer be national economies...."

Actually, what Reich had described had been predicted some time ago. In Snyder's article, "The Revolution in the Workplace: What's Happening to Our Jobs?" in *The Futurist* (March–April 1996), he recalled that

> Most remarkable of all, almost certainly, was sociologist Daniel

Bell's *The Coming of Post-Industrial Society* (1973), which foresaw a society increasingly divided between a small, prosperous technocratic elite and a huge population of lower-middle-income service drones. From the very month it came out, the number of middle-class jobs as a share of all jobs in America fell, just as Bell had projected; it was almost as if he had programmed the economy.

Not only did Bell's prediction come true, but in 1992 the Strategic Studies Institute of the U.S. Army War College published Charles W. Taylor's *A World 2010: A New Order of Nations,* in which he predicted that "the new order of nations almost certainly will evolve gradually into a world economy." He also stated:

> The principal challenges to a national education system that would be the most beneficial for the nation and prepare the people best for the work environment of the world of 2010 are: (1) to create and implement a national education policy that . . . encourages adherence to common standards that ensure equal access to quality education nationwide; (2) to establish comprehensive national education programs. . . .

Remember these when thinking about GATT and GOALS 2000, and note that in Major General William Stofft's (U.S. Army commandant) Foreword to Taylor's book, Stofft indicated that "the author created the concepts for A World 2010 and its forecast in 1984. The narrative was published in a 1986 Army document entitled, *A World 2010: A Decline of Superpower Influence.*"

While the ultimate goal of the global elite is a world socialist government resulting from a dialectical process, what we have recently experienced is perhaps best characterized as "multinational corporatism." Not yet socialism (where government owns at least key industries such as rails, utilities, banking, etc.), but related to fascism (where government controls at least key industries via regulations, etc.), "multinational corporatism" is where large multinational corporations (e.g. Archer-Daniels-Midland in the 1990s) contributed to key politicians (e.g., Bob Dole), who rammed through legislative bodies (e.g., Congress) such things as GATT even though polls showed about eighty percent of the public opposed it.

There is even a book, *When Corporations Rule the World* (1995) by David C. Korten (who was been a Ford Foundation project specialist in Manila) indicating that the emerging global system of business posed a serious threat to long-range human interests. And in an interview with journalist Joan Veon on May 11, 1996, Korten said:

> What we're talking about is the modern extension of the colonial process, colonizing resources, colonizing markets. . . . Internationally, the primary instrument has been the GATT, NAFTA, and now the World Trade Organization (WTO), and essentially the WTO is creating a world government in which one organization which is totally unelected, wholly secretive . . . with the power to virtually override any local or national laws if those in any way inconvenience global corporations. . . . There are new efforts now under way to create new agreements globally which will make it illegal for any country or any locality to give any preference to any local business. . . . It essentially is a process of guaranteeing the rights of global corporations to move anywhere, do anything, without accountability for the consequences. And they systematically drive out the smaller local business that function as part of the community. We see it in the United States, of course, very dramatically in the WAL-MARTS spreading across the country and squeezing out local business, but on a larger scale the same thing is happening in nearly every industry and it's happening throughout the world. . . . It was a terrible shock (to those of us who supported Bill Clinton) when Clinton came in and GATT and NAFTA became the centerpieces of his policy, both for his foreign policy and his domestic employment policy. And in a sense, there was almost a seamless

transition from President Bush to President Clinton in that regard. ... The global financial system and the money that moves unregulated, uncontrolled, through the global system creates a kind of financial referendum that when the folks in power realize that if they do not gear their policies to cater to the international financiers and corporations, that they'll create a run on the currency and with devastating consequences for the economy. The other side of this, of course, is the uncomfortable reality that our democracy has been rendered meaningless by big money. The truth is there are politicians [who] are owned lock, stock and barrel by the big money interests.... Our elections create, to some extent, a façade of choice.... We need to localize economies, not globalize economies ... in a world in which we're protected from others colonizing our resources.

Perhaps one of the "serious threats to long-range human interests" to which Korten referred is the often traumatic results of layoffs occurring under corporate downsizing today. In 1989, William Morin authored *Successful Termination,* giving step-by-step instructions on how to terminate employees, including a checklist of do's and don'ts among which are "do get right to the point" and "don't sympathize." In a 1994 interview with the *Baltimore Sun,* Morin said, "Corporations used to feel guilty about laying people off.... [Now] they have gotten accustomed to terminating people. Their consciences are going away. That's a way of life."

As this global system breaks down national economic barriers, the global elite will argue that a global economy must be managed by a global government. In his book, Knoke affirms that "the foundations to such a reordering have already been laid in the pathbreaking World Trade Organization ... a limited world government with sovereignty over world trade ... [through which] member governments have voluntarily yielded sovereignty over domestic laws governing the environment, food, safety and way of life."

"Voluntarily" yielded? How "voluntary" was it, when Felix Rohatyn testified before the Senate Commerce Committee on November 15, 1994, supporting GATT implementing legislation, and said: "The world financial markets are now more integrated today than the world trading system. . . . The financial markets are assuming ratification of GATT. . . . A change in U.S. attitudes, as represented by a negative vote in the Congress, would carry with it the potential for the most serious consequences in the financial markets"? Rohatyn was a senior partner with Lazard Brothers, and the managing directors of Lazard Brothers until 1963 (Lord Robert Brand) and after 1963 (Adam Morris) both were also heads of the Round Table Groups, formed to further Cecil Rhodes' plan to dominate the world.

And concerning the possibility that the U.N. will evolve into the world socialist government, Knoke advocated that the U.N. be given taxing authority, a standing army, and "a world police force with special training and equipment usually not found in armies." He further advocated that the U.N. have "peacekeepers" who are "a combination of social worker, policeman, riot police, and Rambo-style SWAT commandos." Welcome to the "Bold New World"!

Former CIA director William Colby (who disappeared and was found dead) told John DeCamp: "Sometimes there are forces too powerful for us to whip them individually, in the time frame that we would like. . . . The best we might be able to do sometimes, is to point out the truth and then step aside. That is where I think you are now. For your own personal safety and survival, step aside." Think about what it would take for the former head of the CIA, with all of its resources and power, to say, "there are forces too powerful" and "for your own personal safety and survival, step aside"!

# The Power Elite and the Muslim Brotherhood

Power Elite (PE) agent Lord Herbert Samuel was one of the first to refer to the establishment of a "new world order" (House of Lords, May 16 and August 7, 1918). As a member of the Milner Group that controlled British foreign affairs from the beginning of the twentieth century until WWII, Samuel in 1921 appointed Hajj Amin al-Husseini as mufti and head political administrator of Arab Palestine. Lord Alfred Milner, who was in charge of executing PE member Cecil Rhodes' secret "scheme to take the government of the whole world," on June 27, 1923, in the House of Lords said regarding Palestine that there "must always remain not an Arab country or a Jewish country, but . . . an international country in which all the world has a special interest—I think some Mandatory Power will always be required."

While al-Husseini was in Palestine, Hassan al-Banna founded the Muslim Brotherhood (MB) in Egypt in 1928, and it has been from this organization that radical Islamic groups such as Hamas, Islamic Jihad, and al-Qaeda have come (Mark Hosenball and Michael Isikoff of *Newsweek* have reported connections between al-Qaeda and MB members Mamoun Darkazanli and Youssef Nada). Former CIA agent Robert Baer in *Sleeping With the Devil* explained how the U.S. "made common cause with the [Muslim] Brothers" and used them "to do our dirty work in Yemen, Afghanistan and plenty of other places."

In the 1930s, the MB supported Adolph Hitler (distributing his

*Mein Kampf*), and by 1936 with only eight hundred members began to oppose British rule in Egypt. By 1938, the MB's membership had grown to two hundred thousand, and by the late 1940s to at least a half million.

In 1933, when Adolph Hitler came to power in Germany, Young Egypt (Green Shirts) was also founded in October of that year by Ahmed Hussein who had been greatly influenced by al-Husseini. Young Egypt supported Hitler and the Nazis, and one of its early members was Anwar Sadat who helped the Nazis during WWII. In a September 18, 1953, letter to the Egyptian news daily -*Al-Mussawar*, he expressed his admiration for Hitler.

During WWII, President Roosevelt was no real friend of the Jews. In secretary of state Edward Stettinius' papers, he wrote that during FDR's meeting with Stalin at Yalta (February 4–11, 1945), Stalin asked FDR if he intended to make any concessions to King Saud of Saudi Arabia. And then Stettinius wrote: "The President replied that there was only one concession he thought he might offer, and that was to give him the six million Jews in the United States." The outrageousness of this remark by FDR is perhaps rivaled only by the hypocrisy of his "Day of Infamy" speech regarding the Japanese attack on Pearl Harbor on December 7, 1941, because two weeks earlier (November 25) he had talked with secretary of war Henry Stimson about how they "should maneuver them [Japan] into the position of firing the first shot"! This quote comes from the diary of Stimson, who was a Council on Foreign Relations member as well as the Skull & Bones member who initiated George H. W. Bush into the same Yale University secret society.

After WWII, Gamal Abdel Nasser (a leader of Young Egypt) led the July 1952 coup against the monarchy in Egypt, becoming president in 1956. At first, the CIA indirectly supported Nasser. In *The Game of Nations*, CIA agent (in Egypt) Miles Copeland revealed the agency subcontracted more than one hundred Nazi specialists in security and interrogation techniques to help Nasser. However, as

Nasser grew stronger, CIA director Allen Dulles saw him as a threat who could ally Arabs and Muslims far beyond Egyptian national boundaries. Copeland said Dulles told him, "If that Colonel [Nasser] of yours pushes us too far, we will break him in half."

The MB had originally supported Nasser, and the 1952 revolt, but they became disenchanted with him when it became apparent he would not establish an Islamic state. They were blamed for an assassination attempt on him in 1954, and according to Copeland, interrogations of MB members after the attempt revealed they were merely a "guild" that fulfilled the goals of Western interests: "Nor was that all. Sound beatings of the Muslim Brotherhood organizers who had been arrested revealed that the organization had been thoroughly penetrated, at the top, by the British, American, French and Soviet intelligence services, any one of which could either make active use of it or blow it up, whichever best suited its purposes."

On the book jacket for *Devil's Game: How the United States Helped Unleash Fundamentalist Islam* (2005) by Robert Dreyfuss, one reads:

> Among the hidden stories of U.S. collusion with radical Islam that Dreyfuss reveals here are President Eisenhower's 1953 Oval Office meeting with a leader of the Muslim Brotherhood, and the United States' later alliance with that group and their Saudi patrons against Egypt's President Nasser. Dreyfuss meticulously documents the CIA's funding of the Iranian ayatollahs in the *coup d'état* that restored Iran's shah to power, the United States' support for Saudi Arabia's efforts to create a worldwide Islamic bloc as an antidote to Arab nationalism, and the longstanding ties between Islamic fundamentalists and the leading banks of the West. With clarity and rigor, Dreyfuss also chronicles how the United States looked the other way when Israel's secret service supported the creation of the radical Palestinian group Hamas. . . . *Devil's Game* reveals a history of double-dealing and cynical exploitation that continues to this day—as in Iraq, where the United States is backing radical

Islamists, allied with Iran's clerics, who have surfaced as the dominant force in the post-Saddam Hussein Iraqi government.

The Saudis were opposed to Nasser and became the primary supporters of the MB on the Arabian peninsula and beyond. According to author Martin Lee in *Razor Magazine* (2004), MB members were

> employed as teachers and imams in Saudi mosques, schools and government agencies, where they promoted the extremist doctrine of Sayyid Qutb, the Brotherhood's leading scribe and theorist . . . [who] provided a Koranic justification for violence . . . [against] corrupting Western influences. . . . One of [Osama] bin Laden's instructors in religious studies was . . . the exiled brother of Sayyid Qutb, who taught classes on the imperatives and nuances of Islamic jihad. . . . Muslim Brotherhood veterans have played a prominent role during every phase of bin Laden's terrorist odyssey.
>
> As a college student he was mentored by Abdullah Azzam, a Palestinian [Muslim] Brother. . . . Bin Laden transferred his base of operations to the Sudan in 1991. For the next five years, bin Laden and his inner circle were holed up in Khartoum courtesy of Sheikh Hassan al-Turabi, the Sorbonne-educated head of the Muslim Brotherhood's Sudanese branch. . . . Bin Laden [went] back to Afghanistan in 1996. . . . [Al-Qaeda member] Khalid Sheikh Mohammed . . . self-described mastermind of the 9/11 operation . . . cut his teeth on the Kuwaiti chapter of the Muslim Brotherhood.

Gamal Abdel Nasser was suspicious of American actions as they facilitated the plans of the Power Elite when in 1957, he said: "The genius of you Americans is that you never make clear-cut stupid moves, only complicated stupid moves, which make us wonder at the possibility that there may be something we are missing." Nasser died in 1970 and was followed as president of Egypt by Anwar Sadat, who initially sought the support of the MB but was assassinated by the Islamic Jihad (led by Dr. Ayman al-Zawahiri, former MB member and now the new leader of al-Qaeda) and others on October 6, 1981, after signing a peace treaty with Israel in 1979. Sadat was followed by Hosni Mubarak, who in 2005 began to crack down on the MB after they won twenty percent of the seats in Parliament.

Mubarak was ousted in 2011 with the support of the MB, and in a January 28, 2011, *The [London] Telegraph* article about "America's Secret Backing for Rebel Leaders Behind Uprising" in Egypt, it revealed the leaders "have been planning 'regime change' for the past three years." The article also contains a link to a "secret document." The revolution in Egypt brought with it the return of the MB advisor Yusuf al-Qaradawi after thirty years of semi-exile. This was after British conservative leader David Cameron in January 2008 called for a ban on "preachers of hate," including al-Qaradawi, from entering the United Kingdom. On December 17, 2010, al-Qaradawi said the MB "sanctioned martyrdom operations in Palestine. . . . They do not have bombs, so they turn themselves into bombs. This is a necessity."

According to *The Jerusalem Post* (May 26, 2011), the news daily *Al-Masry Al-Youm* said an Egyptian Nazi Party "operated secretly" under Mubarak "whose regime prevented party leaders from carrying out their activities freely." The same news daily reported that the Nazi Party's founding deputy there "is a former military official," and that the party would be more open and aimed at bringing "together prominent figures from the Egyptian society."

Martin Lee in *Razor Magazine* (2004) also revealed that "pursuant to their long-term strategy of using peaceful means to turn Egypt into an Islamic republic, the Muslim Brotherhood have taken over numerous trade unions and professional associations, while operating banks, businesses, health clinics, schools, and legal services that often outperform shabby government institutions." The MB has chapters in eighty countries and more than three hundred thousand members throughout Egypt. Remember also that 9/11 ringleader Mohammed Atta was an Egyptian and a member of the Engineers Syndicate there which was controlled by the MB.

In a Council on Foreign Relations (CFR) February 3, 2011, backgrounder titled "Egypt's Muslim Brotherhood," one reads that CFR senior fellow Ed Husain believes that Egypt could go the way of Iran, saying: "Then [in Iran], secular democrats triggered a revolution only to be brushed aside by fundamentalists. Today, ordinary Egyptians lead demonstrations, but the Brotherhood waits in the background, an indispensable force in national life. . . . Without the Muslim Brotherhood, there's no legitimacy to whatever happens in Egypt." The backgrounder also indicates that terrorism expert Lydia Khalil explains that MB hardliner elected to Egypt's parliament, Ragib Hilal Hamida, as recently as 2006 "voiced support for terrorism in the face of Western occupation."

According to a report in *Al-Masry Al-Youm* in late June 2011, "Experts in Islamist movements have said they believe Islamic thinker Muhammad Selim el-Awa, an Egyptian presidential hopeful, is the undeclared nominee for the Muslim Brotherhood." And about the same time, former Egyptian MB supreme guide Mohammed Mahdi Akef told *The New York Times* that the MB will reveal its "full platform" when it has won the Egyptian presidency and is in complete control of that nation.

According to *Israel News Update* (July 6, 2011), former CIA director Mike Hayden says he believes the MB could "enjoy a disproportionate power in shaping the new government" in Egypt; and the MB, "which originally said it does not intend to field a candidate for president, has since created a broad supercoalition of opposition parties in hopes of taking Egypt's next government by storm." The result, according to *Jerusalem Post* reporter Caroline Glick in a June 25, 2011, Steel-On-Steel radio interview, is that the MB "is likely to win a governing majority in the next Parliament and control the next president" in the upcoming September 2011 elections.

In Egypt's Arabic press, the MB advocates sharia law. Egyptian Arabic daily *Al-Masry Al-Youm* quoted Sobhi Saleh of the MB as saying "terms like civil or secular state are misleading. Islamic sharia is the best system for Muslims and non-Muslims."

Concerning the recent revolutions in Egypt, Tunisia, Libya, Yemen, etc., they have been marked by violence. Relevant to this, Zbigniew Brzezinski (an advisor to both presidents Jimmy Carter and Barack Obama) in *The Grand Chessboard* (1997) explained the importance of "how the United States both manipulates and manages Eurasia's key geopolitical pivots," and then he revealed: "A possible challenge to American primacy from Islamic fundamentalism could be part of the problem in this unstable region . . . and would be likely to express itself through diffuse violence."

The deputy leader of the MB declared they would try to dissolve Egypt's thirty-two–year treaty with Israel, within which Raed Salah is the MB leader. And if the MB gains control over Egypt, they could coerce Israel into making compromises with its security by blocking the Suez Canal and the narrow Straits of Tiran between the Arabian and Sinai peninsulas. In late June of 2008, Reuters reported that about eight thousand "activists from Jordan's mainstream Muslim Brotherhood" marched through the Jordanian capital calling for more suicide bombings and rocket attacks against Israel in order to destroy the Jewish nation. More recently, in the June 16, 2011, *Global Muslim Brotherhood Daily Report,* one reads that Kuwaiti MB leader Tareq Sweidan told Al-Quds TV that the Islamic "nation" should provide "direct support to the armed resistance" against Israel and that Islamic youth should undertake "electronic Jihad" to destroy Israeli websites. In 2005 and 2007, MB supreme guide Mohammed Akef explained that "as far as the [MB] movement is concerned, Israel is a Zionist entity occupying holy Arab and Islamic lands . . . and we will get rid of it no matter how long it takes."

Concerns regarding the threat posed by the MB are also evident in the Middle East, as Dubai's (United Arab Emirates, UAE) police chief, Lt. Gen. Dahi Khalfan, claimed on March 25 that the "Brotherhood was plotting to change the regimes in the Gulf [Bahrain, Kuwait, Oman, Qatar, Saudi Arabia, and the United Arab

Emirates]. My sources say the next step is to make Gulf governments [their ruling families] figurehead bodies only without actual ruling. The start will be in Kuwait in 2013 and in other Gulf states in 2016." Relevant to Saudi Arabia in this regard, some Saudi leaders "have accused the Brotherhood of inspiring the kingdom's main domestic opponents group, the Salwa movement that in the 1990s agitated to bring democracy to Saudi Arabia" (see "Rise of Muslim Brotherhood frays ties," *Al-Arabiya News*, May 1, 2012).

A February 28, 2013, WorldTribune.com article reported that an MB defector on February 24 told a conference in Abu Dhabi (UAE) that "the Brotherhood, with headquarters in Egypt, was infiltrating Western and Arab states by recruiting their Muslim citizens." The defector, Tharwat Al-Kherbawy,

> said the Brotherhood established secret societies in more than eighty countries, with recruits pledged to violence. The Brotherhood has rejected loyalty to any host country. The Brotherhood presence in any country consists of three units. They included a unit composed of local residents, a secret Egyptian cell, and an international group that reports to superiors in the American city of New York.

UAE foreign minister Abdullah Bin Zayed said the MB "does not believe in the sovereignty of the state," according to the article, which also indicated that "in late 2012, the UAE reported the arrest of ninety-four suspected Brotherhood members accused of trying to overthrow the Gulf Co-orporation Council state. Officials said the Brotherhood marked a leading threat to the UAE as well as such neighboring states as Kuwait."

Lt. Gen. Khalfan's assessment above came the day after the MB's Freedom and Justice Party (FJP) in Egypt questioned whether the Egyptian military's support for prime minister Kamal al-Ganzouri's cabinet (considered a failure by the MB) was due to "a desire to abort the revolution and destroy the people's belief in their ability to achieve their goals? Or is there an intention to defraud or influence the forthcoming [May 23–24, 2012] presidential election?" Further evidence of the power or influence of the MB in Egyptian politics came several days later (March 28) when the constituent assembly (charged with drafting Egypt's new constitution) elected as its head Saad al-Katatni, an MB member and current speaker of the Egyptian parliament.

To allay public fears regarding the MB dominating the political process, the Brotherhood originally declared it would not field a presidential candidate. However, faced with the prospect of having a candidate winning who wouldn't be acceptable to them (or beholden to them) politically or religiously, on March 31, 2012, the MB announced its deputy chairman, Khairat al-Shater (leading MB financier), would run for president. The reason the MB gave for announcing its own presidential candidate was that it felt forced to do so because of "threats to the Egyptian revolution," including the intransigence of the ruling military council in supporting al-Ganzouri's interim government, which the MB felt had been a failure.

The reaction by many to this decision by the MB was one of alarm. On April 3 the head of the liberal Free Egyptians Party, Ahmed Said, questioned: "If al-Shater is president, will he rule in the name of the people or according to the orders of the Brotherhood?" The answer to this question was no small matter, because as Associated Press reporter Sarah El-Deeb wrote on April 3: "A female Brotherhood lawmaker caused a stir by speaking out against the four-year-old ban on female genital mutilation." The same day, al-Shater gave an indication of how he would rule by stating that implementing the sharia (Islamic law) was "his first and final goal." The FJP quickly sought to allay public fears about this by announcing this did not mean a "theocracy" ruled by religious men, and that Christians and Jews would be protected, though only Muslim men can rule. Much of this became moot a few days later when the Egyptian election commission on April 14 disqualified al-Shater due to a past criminal conviction (the MB had been outlawed under President Mubarak).

Concerning the recent so-called spontaneous democratic revolutions in the Middle East and North Africa, as I have written previously, the MB was behind most of these. When there are exceptions, such as The Alliance of National Forces (ANF) candidate Mahmoud Jibril (not an MB member) winning in Libya's July 7 election, one should take note of the fact that just like Mohamed Morsi (the MB's candidate) in Egypt, Jibril is American-educated (and perhaps an intelligence "asset"), and reportedly led the plot to bring down Pan Am flight 103!

In Egypt on June 14, 2012, the Supreme Constitutional Court annulled the Islamist-dominated parliamentary election results, and the military council via constitutional decree gave itself the power to legislate, control the budget, and limit the future president's powers until a new parliament is elected (which may take several months). The MB's Freedom and Justice Party rejected the dissolution of the parliament, thus beginning a showdown with the military council.

According the David Ignatius in the *Lebanon Daily Star* (June 18, 2012), the U.S. government actually saw Khairat al-Shater (the leading strategist of the MB) as "the likely power behind the mild-mannered Morsi." And Caroline Glick in the *Jewish World Review* (June 22, 2012) assessed that the MB had already outmaneuvered the Egyptian military, and "the inevitability of the Islamic takeover of Egypt means that the peace between Israel and Egypt is meaningless. . . . In their attempt to maintain their power and privilege, the first bargaining chip the generals will sacrifice is their support for the peace with Israel."

Morsi won the presidential runoff election on June 24, 2012, and in the president-elect's first public speech on June 29 he promised to work to free Omar Abdul Rahman (known as the "blind sheikh"), who was the spiritual leader of those convicted in the 1993 World Trade Center bombing. Despite this pronouncement, President Obama invited Morsi to come to Washington for a September meeting. Surely Obama also knows that the MB's supreme leader, Mohammed Badi, in a recent weekly sermon "called on all Muslims to wage jihad with their money and their selves to free al-Quds [Jerusalem]" and "save it from the hands of the rapists [Israelis]. . . ." In 2010, Morsi had asked Egyptians to "nurse our children and grandchildren on hatred [of Jews and Zionists]" and a few months later in a television interview described Zionists as "the descendants of apes and pigs." The source for this is a January 15, 2013, Associated Press article regarding Morsi by Matthew Lee and Josh Lederman, who ended their article by writing that the ME "is fiercely anti-Israel and anti-U.S."

After Morsi on June 30, 2012, was sworn in as president, on July 8 he recalled the dissolved parliament to meet. On July 10 they met, but on the same day, Egypt's Supreme Constitutional Court overruled Morsi's decision to reconvene parliament. The last paragraph of "Egypt's parliament reconvenes as new crisis looms between Morsi and judiciary" (*Al-Arabiya News,* July 10 , 2012) states: "The dispute over the fate of parliament has divided the nation just as Egyptians were looking forward to a semblance of stability after the tumult of the last seventeen months since the ouster of longtime authoritarian ruler Hosni Mubarak. Egypt has seen a dramatic surge in crime, deadly street protests, a faltering economy and seemingly non-stop strikes, sit-ins and demonstrations."

Ali Younes (a journalist and writer based in Washington, D.C.) in "Military council and constitutional court pose threat to democracy in Egypt" (*Al-Arabiya News,* July 16 , 2012) pointed out that the Supreme Constitutional Court, the Supreme Military Council, and the state-owned media "were appointed by the previous Mubarak regime." Younes claims that

> the Court and the Military leaders are united in their mortal fear, over their interests and perks, of the Muslim Brotherhood organization which dominates the Parliament and won the presidency.
>
> Morsi's greatest sin is that he is an Islamist from the opposition who defeated their candidate Ahmed Shafiq, an ally and old guard from the Mubarak regime. This decision would be akin to

the U.S. Supreme Court, relying on the 1857 decision in *Dred Scott v. Sanford*, to declare the presidency of Barack Obama illegal and unconstitutional because he is black, and therefore non-citizen, and then proceed to dissolve the current Congress because it was elected while Obama, being black, was president. . . . In Egypt, the Judges were appointed by the Mubarak family as rewards and favors to their friends and allies. . . . Egyptian columnist Farrag Ismail (a mainstream well-known writer who is not an Islamist) wrote in *Al-Gumbouriya* newspaper that "Mubarak still essentially rules Egypt through his cronies who fill the state media, the courts system and the military."

A key agent of the PE has been Zbigniew Brzezinski (ZB). Previously, I explained his facilitation of the Ayatollah Khomeini's replacement of the Shah of Iran almost twenty-five years ago. And in keeping with the PE's long-range plans, ZB in a recent interview with Newsmax (July 18) warned that "a war [with Iran] in the Middle East, in the present context, may last for years. And the economic consequences of it are going to be devastating for the average American—high inflation, instability, insecurity. Probably significant isolation for the United States in the world scene. . . ."

The PE's plan is not for a massive war in the region, but rather a gradual takeover by the MB. Relevant to the MB, on June 12, 2012, U.S. Representative Michele Bachmann and four other members of Congress sent letters to the inspectors-general at the departments of Defense, Homeland Security, Justice, and State, and the director of National Security requesting information regarding the influence of the MB inside the U.S. government. One of the individuals about whom there is concern is Huma Abedin (deputy chief of staff to secretary of state Hillary Clinton), whose mother, father, and brother have connections to organizations with ties to the MB.

The State Department's own guidelines regarding security concerns includes the following: "contact with a foreign family member

... if that contact creates a heightened risk of foreign exploitation, inducement, manipulation, pressure or coercion," and "connections to a foreign person, group, government, or country that create a potential conflict of interest between the individual's obligation to protect sensitive information or technology and the individual's desire to help a foreign person, group, or country by providing that information. ..." The word "potential" here is important.

Representative Bachmann *et al* have been criticized for their efforts not only by President Obama and Hillary Clinton, but also by some leading Republicans (Senator John McCain and House Speaker John Boehner). It is a fact, though, that Huma Abedin as recently as 2008 was an assistant editor of the Institute of Muslim Minority Affairs' journal, and the Institute published a book by her mother, Dr. Saleha Abedin, who is a member of the Muslim Sisterhood.

In Egypt, the next important event was the writing of a new constitution, which would deal with the powers of the president, parliament, and military, as well as the role of Islam. On July 30, 2012, a court deferred until late September a decision on whether to disband the hundred-member Islamist-led constituent assembly which is charged with writing the new constitution. This was considered a victory for the MB, as the assembly can now continue to work on the constitution.

What seems to be occurring is what I predicted—a temporary accommodation between the MB and the military. One by one, the older members of the military leadership will retire (in luxury, perhaps to the Riviera), and the MB will gain more and more control. Signs of such an accommodation were that President Mohammed Morsi's new cabinet, sworn in on August 2, 2012, included Field Marshal Hussein Tantawi as defense minister, and two other generals were minister of the interior (which covers the police) and minister of local government.

Even when Tantawi resigned a few days later, he and his chief-of-staff, Lt. Gen. Sami Anan, were given the nation's highest medal (the Nile Medal) by Morsi. Then Morsi on August 12 replaced Tantawi with Abdel Fattah al-Sissi, who had been chief of Egyptian military intelligence and, according to U.S. secretary of defense Leon Panetta on August 14, "expressed his unwavering commitment to the U.S.-Egypt military-to-military relationship."

As *Time* magazine (August 27, 2012) noted, Morsi's dismissal of Tantawi and Anan

> may not be the dawn of a new era that it appears. Many analysts say the President [Morsi] and the powerful Muslim Brotherhood Islamist party that backs him are not so much cleaning house as just lining up new allies. "Morsi doesn't want to undermine these institutions (e.g., the military). He wants them to be loyal to himself and the Brotherhood," says Robert Springborg, an expert on the Egyptian military and a professor at the Naval Postgraduate School in California.

The Supreme Council of the Armed Forces also was exercising legislative powers instead of parliament (which was dissolved by the court), as well as drafting and passing bills in cooperation with President Morsi until he canceled the constitutional declaration that had given the military legislative and other powers. As Amr Adly wrote in Ahram Online (August 3, 2012):

> The process drafting Egypt's new constitution seems to be subject to the same logic of cohabitation between the old interests and the rising Brotherhood elite. Articles and clauses have been leaked guaranteeing a special status for the military in the new post-Mubarak order. Talk has spread about accepting the existence of the National Defense Council to be the *de facto* ruler on issues of national security and foreign policy. What appears to be actually happening is that the post-Mubarak order will be no more than the rules of mutual accommodation and coexistence between the old powerful interests composed of, on the one hand, the military council, the intelligence and the business oligarchs, and on the other, the Muslim Brotherhood.

However, Adly warned that

> if the Brothers strike a deal with the old interests as the basis for the post-Mubarak order, then very little room will be left for them to deliver any meaningful change. The Brothers reached power in the aftermath of an overwhelming popular uprising that enfranchised broad constitutional yearning for socioeconomic and political change. Change and meeting the revolution's demands were the basic theme of Morsi's campaign in the second round against Ahmed Shafiq, who was branded as the representative of the old regime. If such a scenario materializes, the Brothers will be bound to lose credibility and popularity to more radical actors, be they to the right or to the left.

That is why I didn't believe the situation would remain static for long, as evidenced by Morsi's replacement of Tantawi and Morsi's cancellation of the constitutional declaration giving the military legislative and other powers. Therefore, one can expect the MB initially to focus on improving Egypt's economy, then noticeably gain more power over the next several years as the older military generals retire, and finally implement sharia law.

Earlier, I mentioned that U.S. Representative Michele Bachmann and four other members of Congress had inquired about the possible influence of the MB within our federal government. Representative Keith Ellison asked Representative Bachmann for more information about her concerns, and she replied that the federal government continues to be "advised by organizations and individuals that the U.S. government itself has identified in federal courts as fronts for the international Muslim Brotherhood."

As David Horowitz noted on August 30, 2012: "In 2010, State Department officials began 'engaging' with Muslim Brotherhood representatives shortly before the 'Arab Spring.' In 2011, State Department officials trained Muslim Brotherhood operatives on how to win elections as part of a course in 'democracy theories' following the fall of Hosni Mubarak...."

Earlier, I mentioned that Secretary of State Hillary Clinton's deputy chief-of-staff Huma Abedin's father, mother, and brother have connections to organizations with ties to the MB. In the 1990s at George Washington University, Huma herself was a member of the Muslim Students Association, which has ties to the MB. Not only is Huma's mother a member of the Muslim Sisterhood, but it is worth noting that the wife of the newly elected Egyptian president Mohammed Morsi is also a member of the Sisterhood.

Earlier I indicated my belief that the MB ultimately will institute sharia (Islamic) law throughout Egypt. In the spring of 2012, Morsi emphasized the MB's motto, which states: "The Koran is our constitution. The Prophet Mohammed is our leader. Jihad is our path. And death for the sake of Allah is our most lofty aspiration." According to Reuters' reporter Tom Perry in "Brotherhood man promises Islamic law in Egypt" (May 25, 2012), Morsi declared at one campaign rally: "It was for the sake of Islamic sharia that men were ... thrown into prison. Their blood and existence rests on our shoulders now. We will work together to realize their dream of implementing sharia." Being a pragmatic politician who needed support beyond the MB to be elected president, Morsi pledged to Gama'a al-Islamiya to work for the release of their spiritual leader, Sheikh Omar Abdul Rahman (the blind sheikh imprisoned in North Carolina for his involvement in the 1993 attack on the World Trade Center).

In December 2011, MB supreme guide and leader Mohammed Badi declared there are six phases to their methodology, beginning with sharia law on the individual level and ending with "mastership of the world." Relevant to this, Ryan Mauro (radicalislam.org) on June 27, 2012, reported that a secret meeting of the MB's leadership was held in mid-June resulting in the "Jazira Plan" to implement sharia not only in Egypt, but across a caliphate (MB affiliate Islah already dominates Yemen, and Qatar is subsidizing the MB).

The plan reportedly was approved by Badi, and among its first steps was "replace the national anthem with the so-called anthem of the Islamic caliphate."

Mauro also reported that at one campaign rally for Morsi, cleric Safwat Hegazy announced, "We are seeing the dream of the Islamic Caliphate coming true at the hands of Mohammed Morsi," and "The capital of the Caliphate and the United Arab States is Jerusalem, God willing." It is worth noting, though, that in the struggle for power in the Muslim world, the Sunni MB's desire for a caliphate under its domination is being countered by the "Shiite Crescent" plan of Iran under its domination.

What might life be like under sharia law? Don't count on freedom of the press! An August 9, 2012, report by El-Balad (an Egyptian website read by many) revealed that on the day before, "thousands of the Muslim Brotherhood's supporters" attacked 6-October's media facilities, beat Khalid Salah—chief editor of the privately owned and secular *Youm-7* newspaper—prevented Yusif al-Hassani (a TV broadcaster) from entering the building and generally "terrorized the employees."

Too often, this type of violence goes uncondemned and unpunished, and the more radical elements within Islam (e.g., al-Qaeda) play upon this lack of condemnation to further their terrorist agenda. As Jihad al-Khazen in *Dar Al-Hayat* (August 27, 2012) wrote: "It is therefore the duty of the Muslim Brotherhood in government to combat the terrorism of the deviant faction, and to persuade all Muslims to fight and distance themselves from terrorism and expose their barbaric ideology. . . ."

As I have written before, the PE doesn't like strong national leaders because they might decide to act independently in a way not desired by the PE. Therefore, just as the PE wanted strong nationalists like Mossadegh in Iran removed from power in 1953 and Saddam Hussein removed from power in Iraq more recently, the PE now has decided Bashar al-Assad's time is up in Syria. However, they have not armed the revolutionaries sufficiently to rout his army because they want his removal by negotiated settlement, probably under the auspices of the United Nations.

I have also written how the PE's goal of a world socialist government (WSG) will be achieved by linking regional economic arrangements. This involves revolutions in the Middle East and North Africa bringing most Arab/Muslim nations under the control of the MB. This is why MB leader Mohamed Morsi became president of Egypt. However, because the PE doesn't want strong national leaders, Morsi's recent attempt to decree himself almost dictatorial power was resisted by large protests, and Morsi retreated from his power quest.

Originally, Morsi said his November 22, 2012, decree was to preserve the Egyptian revolution overthrowing Hosni Mubarak. It placed him above judicial oversight so that the constitutional court (CC) appointed by Mubarek couldn't dissolve the panel drafting the new constitution. In April, the CC had dissolved the constitutional assembly which was drafting the constitution, and on June 30 the CC had dissolved the lower house of parliament.

The PE doesn't want the Taliban's extreme interpretation of sharia (Islamic law), and Morsi has endorsed the new constitution's reference to "the principles of sharia" rather than sharia itself. Human Rights Watch, though, "warns that the document is ambiguous on women's rights, allows military trials of civilians and offers no protection for religions beyond Islam, Christianity and Judaism" (*Time,* December 24, 2012). Some of the protests against Morsi's decree had become violent (on December 5, eight were killed and hundreds wounded), but MB lawyer Mohamed Beltagy advised against violence, saying that once the new constitution became law, the people could simply vote the MB out of power, if they wanted, in the parliamentary elections in two months (*Time,* December 24, 2012).

On December 25, Egypt's electoral commission confirmed that by 63.8 percent of the vote (voter turnout was only 32.9 percent), the new constitution was approved. And parliamentary elections would be held by the end of February.

Morsi's opponents were led by Mohamed El-Baradei, and among their grounds for opposing Morsi was that the latter was using the same "torture chambers" as Mubarek did! Egyptian newspaper *Al-Masry Al-Youm* reported: "There are brigades and police officers in military uniforms, as well as others in civilian clothes . . . who oversee the beatings, whippings and torture." Once a protester against Morsi is arrested,

> they ask him why he took to the street, whether he got paid to take part in the protest and whether he supports Mohamed El-Baradei or Hamdeen Sabahi (founder of the Egyptian Popular Current). . . . As long as the person denies the allegations, they beat him and insult his parents. Beatings continued while the victims were transported from the secondary torture chamber to the central one. Many of the prisoners were unable to answer questions after severe beatings, and they were not given medical aid despite bleeding over their entire bodies.

The MB is well organized, though, and extremely practical. Therefore, they will in all likelihood make whatever compromises they have to in order to remain in power in Egypt.

Elsewhere, on January 1, 2013, *Al-Khaleej* (a sharia-based newspaper in the United Arab Emirates, UAE) reported that an Egyptian MB cell of more than ten people had been arrested in the UAE for training local Islamists on how to overthrow Arab governments. Remember that on March 25, 2012, the police chief of Dubai, UAE, Lt. Gen. Dahi Khalfan, claimed that the "Brotherhood was plotting to change the regimes in the Gulf" and that "the start will be in Kuwait in 2013 and in other Gulf states in 2016."

This past October, UAE foreign minister Sheikh Abdullah bin Zayed al-Nahayan said, "The Muslim Brotherhood does not believe in the nation state. It does not believe in the sovereignty of the state." This is why the MB fits perfectly into the PE's ultimate plan for a WSG.

# Looming Economic Disaster

It's a fundamental principal of economics that if one person knows far more than another about a job and will work for much less, that first person will be awarded the job. Currently, relatively few American high school students are taking such subjects as both physics and calculus. However, according to Bob Compton (producer of the DVD "2 Million Minutes"), in China and India about 50 million high school students are taking four years of each of the following: biology, chemistry, and physics, with the senior year integrating all three subjects. Moreover, they take four years each of algebra, geometry, trigonometry, and calculus, with the subjects integrated every year!

Other nations are serious about education, and we are not. At least one high school in China with ten thousand students begins at six a.m. with calisthenics, and students don't leave until ten p.m. This is while American youth seem more interested in playing video games.

What is actually happening is a global transformation to a techno-feudal socialist future, depicted by this photo (see next page) taken recently in China showing a modern skyscraper occupied by a technical or business elite while two women cut the building's grass with scissors. On the one hand, a Chinese company, BYD, after making cars only five years, beat Detroit with the first mass-produced electric car and at only about half the cost. At the same time another Chinese factory making baby clothes for an American company maximizes productivity by incentivizing workers to remain at their work stations

even when they need to go to the restroom (there were no restrooms on site and the place reeked of urine).

Just as American companies have specialized divisions within them, in China entire towns have specialized. Shengzhou produces half the world's neckties, and Putian is the largest tennis shoe manufacturer in the world. One Chinese city, Shenzhen, has a hundred thousand factories producing a majority of the world's laptops, cell phones, jeans, etc. The U.S., however, is losing control over its industries. Amoco's profits go to England; Purina's and Gerber's profits go to Switzerland; and TransAmerica's profits go to The Netherlands. Sound-recording industries here are ninety-seven percent foreign-owned; metal or mining, sixty-five percent; motion picture and video industries, sixty-four percent; book publishers, sixty-three percent; plastic products, fifty-one percent, etc.

Why is all this being allowed to happen? First of all, Americans are woefully ignorant when it comes to economics, and I have covered this in an article on the Internet titled "Suckernomics." Secondly, in an era of globalization, it is almost impossible for Americans to compete with the wages paid to forced or child labor in countries like China, India, Myanmar, Brazil, Bangladesh, and the Philippines. According to a recent CNN report, "The United States has lost a staggering thirty-two percent of its manufacturing jobs since the year 2000. . . . Manufacturing employment in the U.S. computer industry is actually lower in 2010 than it was in 1975."

There has been a plan for some decades to link regional economic arrangements (e.g., the EU, NAFTA, ASEAN) into a world government. As Zbigniew Brzezinski (an advisor to President Obama) revealed at the first State of the World Forum in 1995: "We cannot leap into world government through one quick step. . . . The precondition for eventual and genuine globalization is progressive regionalization because by that we move toward larger, more stable, more cooperative units." Brzezinski was first director of the Trilateral Commission, founded by David Rockefeller who wrote in his *Memoirs* (2002): "Some even believe we are part of a secret cabal working against the best interests of the United States, characterizing my family and me as 'internationalists' conspiring with others around the world to build a more integrated global political and economic structure—one world, if you will. If that's the charge, I stand guilty, and I am proud of it."

In case you think this "one world" concept is only held by a few elites, reflect upon the fact that on June 25, 2001, the U.S. Conference of Mayors endorsed the Earth Charter, which has a goal to "promote the equitable distribution of wealth within nations and among nations," a clearly socialist concept.

Only ten years ago, the U.S. economy was three times the size of China's, but in April 2011 the International Monetary Fund (IMF) forecasted that by 2016 the Chinese economy will surpass that of the U.S. in real terms. Also, by the end of March 2011, China's foreign exchange reserves reached over $3 trillion, but in April 2011 Xia Bin, a member of the monetary policy committee of China's central bank, said they should reduce that by two-thirds to only $1 trillion. This will have a negative impact upon the value of the dollar, which in April fell to its lowest point since 2008.

The U.S. dollar is being devalued as a step on the way to a global currency. On the cover of the January 9, 1988, edition of *The Economist* (next page), you can see a picture of this currency, called "the Phoenix," planned for A.D. 2018. More recently, Robert Fisk wrote "The demise of the dollar" (*The Independent,* October 6, 2009), in which he referred to

> secret meetings [that] have already been held by finance ministers and central bank governors in Russia, China, Japan and Brazil to work on the scheme [to have a basket of currencies for oil], which will mean that oil will no longer be priced in dollars. . . . Chinese financial sources believe President Barack Obama is too busy fixing the U.S. economy to concentrate on the extraordinary implications of the transition from the dollar in nine years' time. The current deadline for the currency transition is 2018.

Similarly, the next year, on September 1, 2010, Dr. Alessandro Sassoli was interviewed by *Coin Update* regarding his idea beginning in 1996 for a new global currency, a project of the United Future World Currency (UFWC) organization. And in this interview, he stated:

"The world is evolving very fast. Maybe in just eight years time, it might be possible to introduce a new super-national currency like the UFWC by 2018."

Thus, the timetable for a world currency by 2018 announced by *The Economist* in 1988 is still proceeding on schedule. And as occultist Alice Bailey in 1933 said, according to "The Plan," the outer structure of the World Federation of Nations will be "taking rapid shape by 2025." This will result ultimately in a synthesis of Western capitalism and Eastern communism into a world socialist government.

# The Election of 2012 ... and the Future

For months, highly paid conservative national talk show hosts like Rush Limbaugh, Sean Hannity, and Glenn Beck were telling us that because of continually high unemployment, etc., there was no way President Obama would be re-elected. On the other hand, for months I have been telling listeners on Radio Liberty that the Power Elite (PE) wanted Obama re-elected in order to be able to fulfill their plan for world control.

The PE wanted Obama to continue to move the U.S. toward socialism as a nation. Remember the 1911 cartoon where PE member John D. Rockefeller is welcoming Karl Marx's socialism to Wall Street. As the U.S. has become more and more socialist, it will be easier to link us to the many other socialist nations around the world in order to form a world socialist government. And as the U.S. becomes socialist as a nation, it will become National Socialist in its orientation (the term NAZI means National Socialist). This is an important aspect of the PE's secret Nazi plan (see my book, *The Power Elite and the Secret Nazi Plan*) coming to fulfillment today.

The Nazis had allied with the Muslim Brotherhood (MB) beginning in the 1930s, and because the PE doesn't like strong nationalist leaders, a pan-Islamic movement and loyalty were created that transcended national borders. As the (international) MB takes over more and more of the countries in the Arab world, it will be easier for the PE to negotiate a regional arrangement with them rather than many national leaders. This regional entity can then be linked with the European Union and other regional entities to form the world socialist government. President Obama's Muslim background will help facilitate this for the PE.

In his post-election day analysis, the supreme self-proclaimed "ego freak," Rush Limbaugh, was so flummoxed that he even contradicted himself by first saying Obama won because you cannot beat (the federal government as gift giver) Santa Claus (Hannity substituted the "permissive parent" for Santa Claus), but then saying Obama won because he wasn't challenged as a liberal by real conservatism. Apparently, the self-proclaimed "all-knowing" Limbaugh doesn't realize that as he defines liberalism, that is Santa Claus! Actually, Limbaugh was closer to the truth than he realized when he jokingly said Obama could have been re-elected by a conspiracy involving George Soros (PE member). You, the readers of this book, should now call your local talk show hosts, and/or write letters to the editors to your local newspapers telling them how Dr. Cuddy correctly predicted the election results while these well-paid, self-assured commentators like Limbaugh, Hannity, and Beck all got the results wrong.

What were the determinative factors in Obama's victory? First, there is what I call Romney's "he's not one of us" characteristic. The two longest serving Republican presidents in the last fifty years were Ronald Reagan and George W. Bush Even though both of them were financially well-off, they both still had a sort of "he's one of us" characteristic. You could actually imagine them in a small town hardware store talking with the locals about the Friday night high school football game. George H. W. Bush didn't have that quality. Richard Nixon (walking along the beach in a suit) didn't have it. And neither did Mitt Romney, even though he has a pleasant personality and has done many kind deeds for needy people.

Secondly, it was assumed that most blacks would vote for Obama, but analysts were surprised that he won the Hispanic vote by about fifty percent, and that fact was characterized as "nationally determinative" in the final election results.

Also, Obama had a sizeable majority of the youth vote. For example, one young conservative analyst on MSNBC said that today's youth were largely supportive of gay marriage as a matter of simple equality for all "humanity." He didn't realize it, but his use of the word "humanity" was telling. It was a religion of humanity that French Revolution supporter Auguste Comte was creating as opposed to the biblically-based values of the American Revolution.

In Comte's humanity religion, each person would decide what is right or wrong for herself or himself based upon the situation, as opposed to automatic and unquestioned obedience to the Word of God which, for example, in Leviticus and Romans declared the wrongness of homosexual behavior. When Bible reading and prayer were forcibly removed from public schools by a government which constantly pounded the moral relativism of non-biblically based situation ethics into students' heads ever since the early 1960s, what else could we expect to happen to our youth?

Two other groups supporting Obama also surprised conservative analysts. Despite the Catholic Church's criticism of what Obamacare would require of Catholic hospitals, etc., fifty-two percent of American Catholics voted for the radically pro-abortion rights Obama! Also, despite President Obama's foreign policies tilting toward Arab-Muslim countries in the Middle East and away from Israel, seventy percent of American Jewish voters cast their ballots for Obama!

In the pundits' post-election analysis, they next said it would be a long time before the Republicans came back. My response is, "No, it won't!" By 2016, many Obama supporters, and perhaps President Obama himself, will wish he had never been re-elected!

By that time, he will face a national and global economy that will be even worse than today. Why? It will be part of the PE's plan to coerce us and the rest of the world into accepting a world currency by 2018. The currency probably will be called "the Phoenix," because it symbolically will be rising from the economic ashes of a failing world economic system. It will be the new global currency of a socialist world economic system that will be managed by the PE's planned world socialist government which will emerge as the "World-State" from a conference in Basra, Iraq, as foretold by Fabian socialist H. G. Wells in his book *The New World Order* (1939).

Who, you might ask, will accept the new world currency for the U.S. in 2018? Just as only a Nixon rather than a Kennedy could establish relations with Communist China about forty years ago, this time only a Bush could get Republicans to accept the loss of American national sovereignty that will come from adopting a single world currency. This is why following Skull & Bones (S&B) member William Whitney's plan in the late 1800s to alternate political power between the Democrats and Republicans, the alternation of power in 2016 (following S&B President George H. W. Bush in 1988, then President Clinton in 1992, then S&B President George W. Bush in 2000, then President Obama in 2008) will see Jeb Bush become president.

How will this happen? Remember that Romney lost the Hispanic vote by about fifty percent in 2012? For his running mate, Jeb Bush could pick Hispanic U.S. senator Marco Rubio from Florida. That should bring in the votes of Hispanics originating from the Caribbean area. Or Bush could pick a Hispanic member of Congress from a highly populated state like California or New York, especially a Hispanic female to attract women voters in general. Also, Jeb Bush is married to a Mexican-born American philanthropist, which should bring in Hispanic votes nationally as well.

The Democratic vice presidential nominee in 2016 will also be Hispanic—perhaps Julian Castro (San Antonio mayor), who delivered the keynote address at the recent Democratic National Convention (a sign the Democrat Party is priming him for national leadership). The problem for the Democratic presidential nominee in 2016 if it's Hillary Clinton (Democrats believe she will clinch the women's vote), though, is the recent attack in Benghazi. Because the

PE wants Jeb Bush to be elected president in 2016, they set Hillary up in Benghazi in a Catch-22 situation to tarnish her reputation for 2016. If Hillary had spoken out that it was the White House and not her State Department which was to blame for the Benghazi disaster, that might have cost President Obama re-election, and Hillary would have been held responsible for the defeat. She therefore grit her teeth and took some of the blame for what happened in Libya, (why didn't she say we shouldn't hire the February 17 Martyrs Brigade to provide security when they "had been implicated in the kidnapping of American citizens as well as threats against U.S. military assets"— April 23, 2013, House Republicans interim report). This will prove to be her downfall in 2016.

Therefore, Vice President Joe Biden may actually be the Democratic presidential nominee in 2016. Telling in this regard is that the day Biden voted in the 2012 election, a reporter asked him if he thought this was the last time he'd be voting for himself for high office, and Biden's response was "No." In 2016, he will be seventy-three years old, but that's the same age Ronald Reagan was when he ran for re-election in 1984. And if Biden is the Democratic presidential nominee in 2016, the PE can count on him to "gaffe" his way to defeat.

But, you may ask, what will be Jeb Bush's campaign themes in 2016? He has already indicated his "moderate" views toward illegal aliens, and that should gain him some Hispanic votes. Plus, he has been heading up an educational enterprise. And by 2016, look for "education" as a subject to be near the top of concerns for the American public.

Jeb Bush's organization is called the Foundation for Excellence in Education, and it has one of these innocuous sounding missions that says it wants to prepare students for "success." I suppose that is better than the "failure" for which our students are currently being prepared. For Bush, this is a nice, safe-sounding, non-specific educational goal that will be hard for Democrats to criticize. After all, it's not identifying, for example, a specific reading program that is supposed to reduce illiteracy by twenty-plus percent.

Thus, the PE's alternation of power will be continued with Jeb Bush's election in 2016. He will "reluctantly" accept the new world currency in 2018, blaming the necessity for doing this on Obama's failed economic policies of the previous eight years. In 2020, with perfect vision (20/20) of the PE's plan, Jeb Bush will win a close re-election, perhaps with an October surprise of a military nature that will persuade the public not to change presidential horses in midstream in a time of crisis (he'll say it's no time for his challenger's on-the-job training). That will make him president until 2024 and time for another alternation of power.

The new Democrat president will take office in 2025, which is the year Luciferian Alice Bailey in 1933 said the World Federation of Nations will be taking "rapid shape" according to "The Plan." The new Democrat president will not only usher in the beginning stages of the PE's planned world socialist government, but also "she" (like Eve in the Garden of Eden) will introduce a New Age/occultic "Angel of Light" spirituality brought by the Light-Bearer (Lucifer, the serpent in the Garden of Eden) for the one-world religion that will accompany the world socialist government. A youth deliberately fed large doses of Harry Potter occultism by then will be middle-aged and in a majority position among the electorate.

That takes care of what will happen in our future. But, you may ask, what will happen next under President Obama? In the future, watch for an important secretly launched military action with specially trained American personnel, who will have a lot of help (including from Israel). It will occur somewhere in the general region from South Asia (Pakistan and Afghanistan) to Iran and the Middle or Near East (including Syria and Yemen) over to North Africa (Libya). The Obama administration will call the operation successful, but it will result in some (manageable) international criticism. Obama's Muslim background will help temper/ease the criticism.

# Looking Backward

[Note: This chapter is written from the perspective of The Order, which by 2100 had come to control the world. Most of this chapter was originally published in 2002 in one of my booklets. Therefore, note that at least one of the predictions came true after that. For example, after 2002 at least one insurance company started adjusting rates on the basis of policyholders doing certain identifiable things to improve their health.]

It is the year 2100 C.E. (Common Era, as A.D. is no longer used), and The Order of the New World or New Civilization has decreed that a history of its rise to power be written by its Ministry of Peace. That is what this paper relates, as we are now living in the most wonderful of times under the guidance of the benevolent Order.

First, it would probably be helpful to describe the model strategy used by The Order to obtain power over the people of the world. Because it was believed that the most difficult people (besides those fervently religious) to bring under The Order's control would be those having a republican form of government, the model strategy used came from Philip Freneau's "Rules for Changing a Limited Republican Government into an Unlimited Hereditary One" (*American Museum*, July 1792), which was an unheeded warning to Americans who supported a republican form of government. This was written shortly after the United States began as a republic, and in this work, Freneau said the limitations of the Republic's (e.g., the U.S.) Constitution should be emphasized with "precedents and phrases" (e.g., due process) "shuffled in." He next said that civil turbulence in the Republic should be contrasted with the stability existing under a hereditary elite. The "grand nostrum" of Freneau's outline was the creation of debt "made as big as possible, as perpetual as possible, in as few hands as possible," and as complicated as possible. He then said, "A great debt will require great taxes. . . . Money will be put under the direction of the government, and government under the direction of money" (e.g., banking elite).

The next step would be to create "artificial divisions" within society (e.g., "divide and conquer" strategy) which would "smother the true natural divisions between the few" (elite) "and the general mass of people, attached to their republican government and republican interests." Freneau then indicated that the elite would give a popular name, such as "the general welfare," to the usurped power so that those opposing the elite could be negatively labeled as "opposing the general welfare" of the people. He described how a military defeat (e.g., the Vietnam War) would "be turned into a political victory for the elite." And lastly, he noted that those warning about the elite's attempt to seize power would themselves be labeled as "enemies to the established government." Freneau declared that this charge would "be reiterated and reverberated till at last such confusion and uncertainty be produced that the people, being not able to find out where the truth lies, withdraw their attention from the contest." This last element of the model strategy was particularly useful to The Order in "turning off" people's support for patriotic militia.

Relevant to this and to the rise of The Order in the twentieth century were the following statements published by the National Education Association's Association for Supervision and Curriculum Development in *To Nurture Humaneness* (1970). Robert Ayres stated that "words like 'patriot' may in time become obsolescent." Dan Dodson noted that "the old order is passing. . . . Social controls cannot be left to blind chance and unplanned change—usually attributed to God. Man must be the builder of new forms of social organization which will be more fulfilling to more people." John Loughary indicated that "many daily decisions and value judgments now made by the individual will soon be made for him." And Raymond Houghton revealed that

> while absolute behavior control is imminent, the crucial question concerns itself with identifying the practical critical factor as to when sufficient behavior control is accomplished to make the question of absolute behavior control only academic. . . . The critical point of behavior control, in effect, is sneaking up on mankind without his self-conscious realization that a crisis is at hand. Man will not ever know that it is about to happen. He will never self-consciously know that it has happened.

As early as May 1966 (in *Esquire* magazine), Dr. James McConnell, professor of psychiatry at the University of Michigan, had been quoted as saying:

> I teach a course called The Psychology of Influence, and I begin it by stating categorically that the time has come when, if you give me any normal human being and a couple of weeks. . . I can change his behavior from what it is not to whatever you want it to be, if it's physically possible. . . . I can turn him from a Christian to a communist. . . . Look, we can do these things. We can control behavior. Now, who's going to decide what's to be done? . . .

Then five years later (September 1971), Milton Rokeach wrote in "Persuasion That Persists" (*Psychology Today*):

> Suppose you could take a group of people, give them a twenty-minute pencil-and-paper task, talk to them for ten to twenty minutes afterward, and thereby produce long-range changes in core values and personal behavior in a significant portion of this group. For openers, it would of course have major implications for education,

government, propaganda, and therapy. . . . My colleagues and I have in the last five years achieved the kinds of results suggested in the first paragraph of this article. . . . It now seems to be within man's power to alter experientially another person's basic values, and to control the direction of the change.

Today, freedom exists under The Order, but it is "managed" for the good of the people. For example, people have a choice in foods to eat, but it is from a selection The Order has determined is healthful for them. Initially, the people had been allowed the illusion of freedom by telling them they could eat whatever they wished. However, if they did not choose from The Order's selection, their insurance premiums were made so prohibitively high that most "volunteered" to choose as The Order desired. It was not difficult to know what each person was eating, as every individual's Omnicard (smart card) recorded what he or she purchased at grocery stores, restaurants, etc. The Order had been able to take control of the world's food supply many decades ago as megafarms bought up nearly all of the small (family) farms, and the megafarms came under the control of giant food processors (e.g., Archer-Daniels-Midland) which in turn were given production quotas by national governments and then by The Order.

In addition to the establishment of criteria for healthful foods, the people happily reported to assigned exercise groups where their physical fitness could be monitored and tracked. Transportation to and from these groups and everywhere else has been accelerated by the development of photon energy, which also powers households and industries. Even space travel is now commonplace because of the development of electromagnetic (EM) power, as EM force fields are emitted by space crafts in front of themselves, accelerating the crafts forward at ever increasing speeds.

The Order was able to begin its movement toward world control over a century ago, before 2000 C.E., by gaining control of the existing "processes." For example, the people were allowed the illusion that they had real political choices during elections, but "big money" from big corporations primarily to Republicans and from big labor primarily to Democrats allowed for the screening of political candidates as they rose on the political ladder to determine if they would be acceptable to The Order. Once computerized voting was introduced, it was also very easy for The Order to program the computers to "rig" election results and to know how everyone voted and whether they voted in a "politically correct" manner. Video cameras showed each person placing his or her ballot in a computer, which clearly displayed the number for each voter (e.g., voter number 49 or 273, etc.) and it was a simple matter for a representative of The Order to retrieve those ballots (e.g., ballot 49 or 273, etc.), from the machine to see how those individuals voted.

Even in the area of education, the credentialing "process" for superintendents, principals, and others became so regulated that even if some disgruntled citizens successfully removed an education official objectionable to them, the official's replacement would have to come from the same pool of "credentialed" educators.

Once the people had come to see that it was useless to challenge The Order (which was, after all, providing for their health, safety, security, and all of their other needs), they came to be dependent upon and to love The Order of the New World. The people's consciousness had been changed so that they have come to accept the New Civilization of the World in which we now live happily. In 1973, feminist leader Gloria Steinem said, "By the year 2000 we will, I hope, raise our children to believe in human potential, not God." This, of course, was accomplished via the establishment of a humanistic code of values to which all could agree, called our common faith. Pope John Paul II's statement supporting the theory of evolution over a hundred years ago helped tremendously in this regard, as it provided much needed support for our undermining of the belief many had in the inerrancy of the Bible. The first head of the World Health Organization, Brock Chisholm, had earlier announced that the concepts of right and wrong taught to children by their parents and religious leaders had to be done away with. And those (e.g., fundamentalists) who objected to this new way of thinking were described as having "mental health" problems which need to be treated by The Order's approved psychiatrists, psychologists, and social service workers.

Once Bible reading and prayer had been removed from public schools, and the public's belief in moral absolutes had been eroded via a steady diet of values clarification lessons in those schools leading to the acceptance of situation ethics, it was not too difficult to gain public acceptance of abortions and other anti-life activities. There was even the election of a president whom the people knew to have committed clearly immoral acts, and to whom a majority of the people gave high approval ratings even though he supported the grotesque infanticide of partial-birth abortions.

The people still longed, though, for some type of spirituality, so unlike the failed communists and Nazis of the previous century, The Order did not try to eliminate the concept of God, but rather redefined God as being the cosmic force of love. This concept of a non-judgmental God who would never send anyone to something called Hell allowed the development of The Order's one-world religion based upon our common faith in the goodness of men and women. Once again, this concept was greatly assisted by Pope John Paul II and other religious leaders who pronounced that Buddhists and those of other religions could also enter into Heaven. The Order's new world religion of common faith based on common values includes a synthesis of Western scientism and Eastern mysticism along with some New Age elements.

Such efforts at syncretism had been tried earlier in the first part of the twentieth century, but had been thwarted by individuals such as G. K. Chesterton who, in *The Everlasting Man* (1925), had written:

> They call a Parliament of Religions [1893] as a reunion of all the peoples; but it is only a reunion of all the prigs. Yet exactly such a

pantheon had been set up two thousand years before by the shores of the Mediterranean; and Christians were invited to set up the image of Jesus side by side with the image of Jupiter, of Mithras, of Osiris, of Atys, or of Ammon. It was the refusal of the Christians that was the turning-point of history. If the Christians had accepted, they and the whole world would have certainly, in a grotesque but exact metaphor, gone to pot. They would all have been boiled down to one lukewarm liquid in that great pot of cosmopolitan corruption in which all the other myths and mysteries were already melting. It was an awful and an appalling escape. Nobody understands the nature of the Church, or the ringing note of the creed descending from antiquity, who does not realize that the world once very nearly died of broad-mindedness and the brotherhood of all religions.

In the latter half of the twentieth century, however, the people were successfully conditioned to compromise their faiths to accept the syncretism of the world's religions.

Because one's religion seemed to matter less and less, people

stopped going to churches, which were turned by The Order into houses of entertainment, as people increasingly seemed to "worship" having fun. Perhaps the first example relevant to this was the conversion of St. John the Baptist Church in the Pittsburgh, Pennsylvania, area to a Brew-pub in the mid-1990s (see photo). The people didn't protest when the music and lyrics from many traditional religious songs (e.g., from Handel's *Messiah,* "The Hallelujah Chorus," and from "God Rest Ye Merry Gentlemen") were used in commercial jingles. The masses of people were kept happy, and formerly illegal drugs were more freely distributed by The Order toward that end. Television, with its quickly changing hyper-reality images (in ads and other programming), and other forms of entertainment became useful in psychologically conditioning the people to accept new lifestyles desired by The Order (centuries ago, yogis had devised candles with a fast flicker effect that could change states of consciousness). Rhythm in music was used to soothe or to stimulate people's emotions, which were now emphasized over the intellect.

Talk show hosts approved by The Order were continuously programmed on radio and television both to allow the venting of frustrations and to mollify fears, reassuring the people that they were still free and had real political choices, naturally within the limits established by The Order for the people's own good. The viewing of sports events continued to be a favorite pastime for the masses, and so that no one team gained superiority in any sport for any length of time, the outcomes of competition were carefully managed by The Order without the public's knowledge.

This did not even require the knowledge of individual players as to what the outcome of any game was to be, as simple signals by representatives of The Order on either side of a court or playing field could alert the opposition as to the appropriate defense to call. It was actually amusing to see how ignorant people had become, as they didn't realize how easy it was to "rig" an athletic event. All it took was one player deliberately missing one shot or kick or catch at a key point in the game!

Because the public always wanted something "new" (similar to the Athenians in the biblical reference of Acts 17:21), "change" was constantly structured into society (e.g., fashions, cars, etc.), and President Barack Obama's theme of "change" in the early twenty-first century helped in this regard. All new cars were then fitted with On-Board Diagnostics III computers (each having its own electronic signature) which The Order could command (by global positioning satellites transmitting signals to the computers) to shut off the engine of anyone attempting to flee The Order's control. The people had already been conditioned to accept the monitoring of their movements when, late in the twentieth century, video cameras were installed on interstate highways, in North Carolina for example, "to obtain information about travel patterns." The cameras recorded license plate numbers, and motorists using many of one metropolitan area's streets and highways were asked at checkpoints about the origin, destination, and purpose of their trips.

As one of the major forerunners of The Order, Bertrand Russell, had stated, "Diet, injections, and injunctions will combine, from a very early age to produce the sort of character and the sort of beliefs that the authorities consider desirable, and any serious criticisms of the powers that be will become psychologically impossible." People also were kept busy so that they did not have time to analyze what was happening to them and possibly resist what The Order was doing for their own good. More and more women were encouraged to go to work to find self-fulfillment, thus enabling The Order to have more and more children placed in its approved daycare centers, where its child-rearing experts could shape the children's values to accept The Order's new world. People had to obtain licenses to become parents, and in order to mold the new man and woman desired by The Order, advanced eugenic projects were conducted based upon earlier research funded by the Rockefeller and Carnegie Foundations. These were based on the philosophy of leading Fabian socialist Sir Julian Huxley who, as first director-general of UNESCO in the previous century, had written in *UNESCO: Its Purpose and Its Philosophy* about the need for a philosophy of "scientific world humanism," about the need to "transfer full sovereignty from separate nations to a world organization . . . political unification in some sort of world government," about the need to promote "a single world culture," and then he stated: "Even though it is quite true that any radical eugenic policy will be for many years politically and psychologically impossible, it will be important for UNESCO to see that the eugenic problem is examined with the greatest care, and that the public mind is informed of the issues at stake so that much that now is unthinkable may at least become thinkable."

The physicians of The Order now routinely replace human organs with the bodily organs of cows, pigs, and baboons. And the doctors laugh amongst themselves as they reflect upon the fact that in the previous century, the people would have expressed outrage if Nazi doctors had performed the same transplants. Coincidentally, as late as 1972 former Nazi SS officer Paul Dickopf directed Interpol, which was begun in the 1920s. Its formation was overseen by Raymond Fosdick who also founded (on behalf of John D. Rockefeller, Jr.) the eugenics-promoting Bureau of Social Hygiene, and who in his memorial history of (Rockefeller's) General Education Board indicated the Board was part of John D. Rockefeller, Jr's effort toward "this goal of social control."

The Order trained Ministers of Euthanasia so that people would not suffer unnecessarily when their usefulness to The Order has ended. This was done by euthanasia chemical compositions patented by Michigan State University. On July 1, 1994, a law firm representing the university declared that the compositions were intended for use in lower animals, but then added: "If it should ever become legal to use the compositions on human beings, the patent claims should encompass the use of compositions of the present invention for this purpose." Funding for the university's research in this project came from Hoechst AG, parent company of Roussel-Uclaf (developer of the

RU-486 abortion pill) and stepchild of I.G. Farben, which manufactured gas for the Nazi concentration camps in the 1940s and had connections with Rockefeller enterprises (John D. Rockefeller III in 1952 founded the Population Council).

Dr. Richard Day (national medical director of Planned Parenthood from 1965 to 1968) in March 1969 had explained that euthanasia would be more accepted as the cost of medical care intentionally would be made burdensomely high. This led to the planned "health care crisis" of the early twenty-first century that facilitated the acceptance of a national health care plan that helped move the U.S. more and more toward socialism.

As another one of the major forerunners of The Order, George Bernard Shaw, had stated: ". . . under socialism you would not be allowed to be poor. You would be forcibly fed, clothed, lodged, taught, and employed whether you liked it or not. If it were discovered that you had not the character and industry enough to be worth all this trouble, you might possibly be executed in a kindly manner. . . ." Shaw's reference to socialism is applicable because The Order manages a world socialist government resulting from a synthesis of Western capitalism and Eastern communism. The experimental model for this synthesis began in July 1997 when Hong Kong (capitalist) was turned over to China (communist), resulting in Hong Kong's synthesis into a socialist government.

Once the people of the world had come to value economic considerations more than moral considerations, The Order's path to power was made much easier. For example, China's human rights violations were deliberately overlooked by national governments, which wanted to maintain their businesses' access to the huge population and markets of China. Not only did national governments overlook China's human rights violations, but the people in general had been conditioned to ignore the fact that many goods in stores were produced by slave or forced labor in China, Russia, Myanmar, Bangladesh, Brazil, the Philippines, etc. Before the American Civil War, the Southern planter class justified enslavement of blacks in the U.S. by saying they were better off than being enslaved or killed by their conquerors in Africa. In the late twentieth and early twenty-first centuries, many Americans justified their benefiting from slave or forced labor in other countries by saying those laborers were better off than they otherwise would have been.

One result of this abandonment of moral considerations was that early in the twenty-first century China became a world economic power and shortly thereafter a world military power with nuclear weapons equal to those of any other nation. With this might, they were able to obtain hegemony over Southeast Asia, take over Taiwan, and threaten Japan and South Korea. This caused an international crisis, resulting in the other nations of the world uniting to resist Chinese expansionism, thus planting the seeds for the acceptance of world government.

Similarly in the areas of economics, a series of international economic crises (e.g., in the fall of 2008 C.E.) caused the nations of the world to unite existing regional economic trading blocs under the already growing authority of the World Trade Organization. A new world financial and monetary system was then established with the "Phoenix" in 2018 C.E. replacing the dollar, yen, and other currencies. All societies became cashless, as smart cards (called Omnicards) were issued to everyone. These were then superseded by the L.U.C.I.D. system's Universal Biometrics Card (UBC) containing information from iris scans, DNA genotyping, and Human Leukocyte Antigen data, all within an International Standardization Organization (ISO) Reference Model. The UBCs also contained each person's education, health, financial, and other records, which were all kept on file at The Order's central databank. It was amusing to see the Christians, who were familiar with the biblical reference to the "mark of the Beast," so willingly accept these UBCs with individually assigned numbers without which they could not buy or sell anything. Biochips were also implanted under everyone's skin at birth so that they would be locatable. And U.S. Patent 5,878,155 approved March 2, 1999, gave The Order a method (a bar code or a design tattooed on an individual) for verifying human identity during electronic sales transactions. It was curious that many Christians went along with this despite the fact that Leviticus 19:28 said: "Ye shall not . . . print any marks upon you: I am the LORD."

Community service acceptable to The Order was required for anyone to obtain employment. Of course, the people were allowed the illusion of freedom by telling them they did not have to engage in such service, but that their admission to higher education and their obtainment of employment were dependent upon their performing this service. Naturally, most "volunteered" to serve. Jobs were appropriately selected for individuals based upon their usefulness to The Order, and employers used Total Quality Management (TQM) principles for which employees had been prepared by school-to-work programs approved by The Order. All students, including those homeschooled or in private schools, were required to pass subjective outcome- or performance-based tests prepared by The Order before they could pursue higher education or be employed. These tests were designed to separate the future elite of The Order from the masses of labor serfs who would perform the service jobs in the techno-feudal society The Order was creating. The concept of "lifelong learning" was used by The Order as another excuse whereby files could be maintained on everyone from cradle to grave. All students had to obtain school-to-work skill certificates, and workers' credentials (demographic and educational/training information, occupational experience, etc., as in the Nazis' Arbeitscbuch or Communist Chinese Dangan) were contained on their UBCs.

Early in the previous century, revolutionary Antonio Gramsci (among whose followers were the last head of the old Soviet Empire, Mikhail Gorbachev, and his wife) theorized that to take control of a nation, one must attack its culture, including education and music. Relevant to education, Marxist philosopher Gyorgy Lukacs (who introduced sex education in Hungary's schools as their commissar for Culture and Education) was admired by Max Horkheimer, who helped found the Institute for Social Research (Frankfurt School) in 1923. Horkheimer developed "critical theory" with the goal of social emancipation, and along with Theodor Adorno and Herbert Marcuse (who coined the phrase "make love, not war") at the Frankfurt School promoted cultural Marxism. They came to New York City and were loosely affiliated with Columbia University (where John Dewey was) from 1934 to 1943. "Critical theory" criticized the traditional values of the cultural institutions in Western capitalist countries. In 1941 Edward Glaser authored *An Experiment in the Development of Critical Thinking*, and The Order was able to use "critical thinking" to foment the "generation gap" in the 1960s. As an educational tool, "critical thinking" was used to cause students to criticize the traditional values of their parents, clergy, and other authority figures.

Relevant to the area of music, Theodor Adorno of the Frankfurt School described how fractious (e.g., rock) music could be used to undermine the traditional values of an existing culture. Paul Cantor of Jefferson Airplane was reported as saying, "The new rock music is intended to broaden the generation gap, alienate parents from their children, and prepare young people for revolution." Similarly, David Crosby (of Crosby, Stills, Nash and Young) said in *Rolling Stone* (vol. 1): "I figured the only thing to do was to steal their kids. . . . I'm just talking about changing young people's value systems which removes them from their parents' world effectively." In education, "forced busing" destroyed the concept of "neighborhood schools" for many, and greatly reduced the ability of parents to be involved in their children's education.

Proponents of "forced busing" relied much upon the research of James Coleman, who wrote in *The Adolescent Society* (1961, research funded by the U.S. Department of Education and the Ford Foundation):

> The adolescent lives more and more in a society of his own; he finds the family a less and less satisfying psychological home. ... Even if a strategy (to bring the adolescents back into the home) were extremely successful, it would have serious disadvantages. ... Equality of opportunity, which becomes ever greater with the weakening of family power, would hardly be possible.

With "forced busing" (which increases the separation of parents from their children) in place to facilitate "equality of opportunity," it was fairly easy for The Order to reduce parents' role in the education of their children even further to the status of being simply one of many "partners." Students, along with the adult population, had come to be considered by The Order as merely its own "human resources," or "human capital," or "humanware."

Once education had been nationalized in all of the countries of the world, it was not difficult for The Order to promote international standards in education as necessary if students were to be prepared to become workers in a global economy. Thus, education became internationalized, and schools everywhere were enlarged to become community service centers, providing not only education but also health care and other social services (e.g., contraceptives, abortion pills, etc). Population control was also maintained by The Order's placement of fertility control agents in the water supply of certain selected communities where labor-serf housing was assigned.

Of course, there were periods when The Order's absolute rule was lessened, even allowing small revolutions to occur, so that potential adversaries to The Order could be drawn out, identified, and dealt with before they could become too great in number. Bertram Gross had explained in *Friendly Fascism: The New Face of Power in America* (1980) how computerized information could be used for "direct character assassination and defamation. ... The creative assembly of unrelated sounds is now possible through electronic means. ... Through 'tape-recording,' a person's own voice may be used to say anything that the tape recorders want him to say." Gross also had described how this might be done in the editing of film and videotapes by "the use of new RAVE methods (Random Access Video Editing)."

In the late twentieth and early twenty-first centuries, the primary opposition to The Order was from various patriot militia groups around the world. The Order wisely engaged in a plan to discredit these groups along with very religious people by branding them as extremists who want to impose their views on everyone else. It was not difficult to infiltrate these groups with agents of The Order, who engaged in such outlandish behavior that the public perception of the patriotic groups to which they belonged became negative. Conveniently, while media and press attention focused upon right-wing militia as a threat to the U.S. government, little notice was given to the International Socialist Organization's (holding regular meetings at universities across the U.S.) promotion of "worker's militia" and its statement that "the struggle for socialism is part of a worldwide struggle. . . . To achieve socialism, the most militant workers must be organized into a revolutionary socialist party. . . . Only mass struggles of the workers themselves can destroy the capitalist system. . . . Capitalism must be overthrown 3. . ." (*Socialist Worker*, November 22, 1996).

So that the people did not recognize and react against The Order's growing power and control, use was made of various psychological techniques. For example, use was made of the work of Wundtian psychologist Kurt Lewin and Soviet psychologist Alexander Luria concerning the artificial disorganization of behavior to control human behavior via the creation of social chaos. Their work was followed by J. R. Rees' "Tavistock Method" inducing and controlling stress in order to make people give up firmly held beliefs under "peer pressure." Rees' work was followed by the "social turbulence" theory of Tavistock senior staff member Fred Emery. Use of this theory by The Order was carried out by creating a series of emotional crises, which caused the people to reduce the tension by adaptation and eventually psychological retreat (similar to Pavlov's "protective inhibition" response), accepting the will of The Order.

"Psychologically controlled environments" (Rees' term) were created to manipulate particular populations via mass media. Relevant to this, villains in films did things so horrible that anything "anti-hero" heroes did to them, the audience would accept it. Modifying this technique, whenever the public began to become suspicious of The Order's growing power, they were flooded with fictional conspiratorial books, motion pictures, and television programs showing life in the future to be so totally controlled and terrible under various "Big Brother" types that they became confused and unable to perceive what The Order was in reality doing gradually to control them. And what the Order was actually doing was viewed by the public as not so extreme when it was compared to the hideous portrayals of the future presented by The Order in these books, films, and TV programs. Thus, the people were psychologically manipulated into non-resistance to The Order's increasing power and control over their lives.

The possibility of terrorism, such as the nearly one hundred missing Russian nuclear devices capable of fitting into suitcases, plus actual terrorist attacks upon buildings, airplanes, trains, etc., were used by The Order to justify greater monitoring of the population's activities along with the confiscation of all firearms. The basis for firearms confiscation was a February 20, 1997, U.S. Justice Department letter indicating the Clinton administration's position that Americans had no Second Amendment constitutional rights as individuals.

Immediately after the terrorist attack against the World Trade Center and the Pentagon on the morning of September 11, 2001, ABC News/*Washington Post* that evening released poll results indicating at least two-thirds of those surveyed "would sacrifice some personal liberties in support of anti-terrorism efforts." This willingness of the people to sacrifice liberties paved the way for passage of the Patriot Act and the Homeland Security Act, both of which infringed upon the people's freedom. Precedent for monitoring people's activities had already been accepted with the U.N. Fourth World Conference on Women in Beijing, China, in 1995, where a "family dependency ratio" was suggested. This ratio would measure each family member's production and consumption to see that it was in line with preserving "sustainable development." The U.N. and World Bank then audited natural capital (natural resources), manufactured capital (anything built), human capital (a person's work skills, etc.), and social capital (what people think). Megachurch pastor Rick Warren, who was mentored by Peter Drucker, was helpful in this regard, as he got all of the churches across the globe on board for this agenda, thereby neutralizing any remaining opposition.

In public areas, video and audio monitors were placed on all streets and buildings; and in people's homes, audio monitors were placed on all phones, and all televisions were adapted for two-way viewing. The public was told that this was to make them secure from theft and assault. Because computer hackers had become so proficient, the public was advised that for their own good, all domestic (including bank transactions) and Internet computer communications would have to be monitored by The Order. All word-processing and e-mail programs, all web browsers, and all computer software contained components allowing The Order to monitor everyone's communications and other activities without their knowledge.

On October 1, 1997, the federal government of the United States began operating a directory of all people hired for any full-time or part-time job in the U.S. All employers were required every three months to report all employees' wages, and the gigantic database also even included the amount of the individuals' assets and debts. Then on the front page of the July 20, 1998, *New York Times,* reporter Sheryl Stolberg wrote: "As legislation that would protect patient privacy languishes in Congress, the Clinton administration is quietly laying plans to assign every American a 'unique health identifier,' a computer code that could be used to create a national database that would track every citizen's medical history from cradle to grave." It was somewhat surprising to see how willing the people were to lose their right to privacy, their right to bear arms, and their freedoms in exchange for the peace, stability, and security provided by The Order.

Late in the previous century, The Order's National Security Agency even developed the ability to monitor individuals' electromagnetic emissions from their brains using remote neural identification and monitoring techniques, and then alter certain individuals' brain waves (based upon capabilities of U.S. Patent 3,951,134, approved April 20, 1976) for their own good or, if necessary, to discredit those who were obstinate and resisted the beneficent work of The Order. Relevant earlier work included IBM's 2020 neural chip implant, tested upon unsuspecting (sedated before implanting) Soledad prisoners, which provided a visual and audio record of all events in which they were involved, and which was used to reduce aggression, to make them lethargic, or to disable them.

In 2025 C.E., this was supplemented by a computer chip (implanted behind the eye) developed by British Telecom's artificial-life team headed by Dr. Chris Winter. This chip records a person's every sensation, which can then be played back by a computer. The Order's capabilities in this regard were an extension of what Zbigniew Brzezinski had written about the earlier Technozoic Era in his book, *Between Two Ages* (1970), in which he stated that

> in the technetronic society the trends seem to be toward . . . effectively exploiting the latest communication techniques to manipulate emotions and control reason. . . . Human beings become increasingly manipulable and malleable . . . the increasing availability of biochemical means of human control . . . the possibility of extensive chemical mind control. . . . A national grid that will integrate existing electronic data banks is already being developed. . . . The projected world information grid. . . .

The Technozoic Era was followed by the Ecozoic Era in which

ecological and environmental concerns were used to persuade people that only a world government could solve the problems in these areas which transcend national borders. Very helpful in this regard were the early efforts of Mikhail Gorbachev, who became head of the International Green Cross, and remarked:

> We are part of the Cosmos. . . . Cosmos is my God. Nature is my God. . . . I believe that the twenty-first century will be the century of the environment, the century when all of us will have to find an answer to how to harmonize relations between man and the rest of Nature. . . . We are part of Nature. . . . The future society will be a totally new civilization which will synthesize the experience of Socialism and Capitalism.

In the Ecozoic Era, the pledge of allegiance to the flag was replaced by the pledge of allegiance to the Earth. One of the pioneering efforts in this regard was Putnam School in Minneapolis, Minnesota, in the early 1990s. This was followed by the U.S. Conference of Mayors on June 25, 2001, endorsing the Earth Charter, which has as a goal to "promote the equitable distribution of wealth within nations and among nations," a clearly socialistic concept. Also, The Order's agents' deliberate placement of endangered species on land desired by The Order was useful as a pretext for confiscating people's property.

At the beginning of this past century, the people had become anxious over the increasing chaos in the world, and they longed for peace, stability, and security. Toward this end, health care, education, service, and even the police of all nations had been nationalized and then internationalized, first under the authority of various U.N. agencies and then under The Order. U.N. treaties (e.g., on children's rights) were enforced through domestic courts in the nations of the world. Military downsizing in nearly all of the nations forced a greater and greater reliance upon U.N. peacekeepers to quell disturbances and even to intervene in advance in countries where there might be trouble (e.g., racial discrimination in the U.S.). The people were already used to U.N. peacekeepers and foreign troops on their own soil, and these forces from other nations were used to put down domestic uprisings, even in the U.S. Eventually nations became borderless, and immigrants moved freely wherever they pleased, with The Order's permission, of course. This resulted in a loss of what had been known as national cultures, and all countries came more and more to resemble each other, forming a new world culture under the benevolent, guiding hand of The Order of the New World or New Civilization.

Relevant to The Order's establishment of a one-world culture, economy, government, and religion, early socialist Auguste Comte had written in *System of Positive Polity* (vols. I–IV, 1851–1854) and *The Catechism of Positive Religion* (translated in 1858) about "the class whose special function it is to systematize man's peaceful activity" and

> a systematic domestic organization of public opinion, as they will stamp an unconstrained uniformity on all the salons of the globe, a process facilitated by the progressive acceleration of all means of communication. . . . Ultimately, political power will fall into the hands of the great leaders of industry. . . . The industrial chiefs are the representatives of Humanity. . . . The principle of all regular concentration of duty is this: A single manager for the whole field of industry which one man can personally direct. Thus temporal authority will be centered in a certain number of Families, scarcely one-thirtieth part of the entire population. . . . Man indeed, as an individual, cannot properly be said to exist. . . . Existence in the true sense can only be predicated of Humanity. . . . Now that Sociology is once for all substituted for Theology as the basis for the religious government of mankind. . . . Everywhere the relative definitively takes the place of the absolute. . . .

With the people thus accepting moral relativism over biblical moral absolutes, The Order was able via a series of crises to create a climate of desperation in which the people became willing to give ultimate power to the leader of The Order in the hope that their problems would be solved. For three and one-half years, The Order's benevolent leader allowed the people to believe they had chosen wisely their ruler. However, for almost the last three and one-half years, The Order's wonderful leader has ruled more forcefully for the public's own good.

Because the people began to see the leader as The Antichrist foretold in what they called The Holy Bible, The Order once again decided to assuage the public's fears by creating their expected second coming of Jesus Christ. Late in the twentieth century, the Intel Corporation had developed a supercomputer capable of performing more than 1 trillion calculations a second. This was described by Intel expert Justin Rattner as "a baby step toward being able to do a real simulation of the physical world," where holographic scenes could not be easily distinguished from reality. After The Order significantly improved upon this "baby step," it holographically portrayed what many believed to be the second coming of Jesus Christ. (Note that Revelation 13–14 repeatedly refer to the "image of the beast," the false Christ.) This helped fulfill in 2100 C.E. "the Plan" foretold by leading occultist Alice Bailey (whose first works were published by Lucifer Publishing) in her pamphlet "The Next Three Years (1934–1935–1936)," in which she described the "outer form" of the "World Federation of Nations . . . taking rapid shape by 2025." She further remarked therein that one should "not infer by this that we shall have a perfected world religion and a complete community of nations . . . but the vision and the idea will be universally recognized, universally desired, and generally worked for. When these conditions exist, nothing can stop the appearance of the ultimate physical form. . . . Approximately four-hundred men and women are working consciously with the Plan."

Further regarding The Order's created perception of Jesus Christ's second coming, late in the twentieth century the sound of a trumpet in midair without the use of a loudspeaker was generated by using

American Technology Corporation's Norris Acoustical Heterodyne Effect, acoustically mixing ultrasonic waves to create new waves that can be heard as sound in "midair." (Note that Revelation 13:15 says that the image of the beast is given "life" and should "speak.")

The pyramid constructed to honor the accomplishments of The Order is now nearly complete as it reaches into the sky, higher than any other structure ever built by man. As I am concluding this paper describing the wonderful history of The Order's rise to power, I am looking out of a window in the Ministry of Peace near the top of the commemorative pyramid and there is lightning in the sky from east to west. There is also a sound like a trumpet filling the air, and in the sky I see a figure of a Man coming. . . .

# Index

**Symbols**

6-October   122
2012 presidential election   8, 131–132

**A**

Abedin, Huma   62, 117, 118, 121
Abedin, Saleha   118
Abel, Jacob   34
*Abington v. Schempp*   24
abortion   21, 25, 27, 30–31, 46–47, 132, 146, 150
Acheson, Dean   82
Adams, John   51
Addison, Alexander
— "Rise and Progress of Revolution"   41
Addison, C. G.
— *Knights Templars, The*   10, 12
Adler, Mortimer
— *Haves Without Have-Nots*   100
Adly, Amr
— Ahram Online   119–120
Adorno, Theodor   149
Ahmad, Mahmoud   70
Akef, Mohammed Mahdi   111–112
*Al-Arabiya News*
— "Egypt's parliament reconvenes as new crisis looms between Morsi and judiciary"   116
— "Rise of Muslim Brotherhood frays ties"   113
al-Assad, Bashar   122
al-Assad, Hafez   66
al-Banna, Hassan   106
Alexander I of Russia   29

Alexander, Lamar   46
Alfred P. Murrah Federal Building   69, 73–75
al-Ganzouri, Kamal   113, 114
al-Hassani, Yusif   122
al-Hussaini, Hussain   71
al-Husseini, Hajj Amin   71, 106–107
al-Islamiya, Gama'a   121
al-Katatni, Saad   114
Al-Khaleej   124
al-Khazen, Jihad
— *Dar Al-Hayat*   122
Al-Kherbawy, Tharwat   113
Alliance of National Forces, The   115
*Al-Masry Al-Youm*   110–111, 124
al-Nahayan, Abdullah bin Zayed   124
al-Qaeda   63, 66, 69–70, 73, 106, 109–110, 122
al-Qaradawi, Yusuf   110
al-Sharia, Ansar   63
al-Shater, Khairat   114, 115
al-Sissi, Abdel Fattah   119
al-Turabi, Hassan   109
al-Zawahiri, Ayman   109
American Civil War   15, 61, 146
American Commission to Negotiate Peace   78
Anan, Sami   118, 119
Antichrist, The   157
Archer-Daniels-Midland   103, 139
Arnaldus, Prior at Sion   10
Aryan Republican Army   73
ASCD. *See* Association for Supervision and Curriculum Development
Assagioli, Robert   60

[ 159 ]

Assassins 9
Association for Supervision and Curriculum Development 97
— *To Nurture Humaneness* 137
Atta, Mohammed 70, 110
Axelrod, Alan
— *International Encyclopedia of Secret Societies and Fraternal Orders, The* 37
Aydelotte, Frank 80
Ayres, Robert 137
Azzam, Abdullah 109

**B**

Babeuf, François-Noël 36
— *Conspiracy of Equals* 37
Bachmann, Michele 117–118, 120
Badi, Mohammed 115, 121–122
Baer, Robert
— *Sleeping With the Devil* 106
Bailey, Alice 20, 27, 38, 96, 129, 135, 157
— "Next Three Years (1934–1935–1936), The" 157
— *Treatise on the Seven Rays: Esoteric Psychology, A* 38
Bank for International Settlements 16–17
Bank of Amsterdam 14
Bank of England 14
Banyan, Will
— "Short History of the Round Table, A—Part I" 37
Barmby, Goodwyn 44
Barrett, Edward
— *Truth Is Our Weapon* 91
Barruel, Abbe
— *Antisocial Conspiracy* 42
Barruel, Augustin
— *Memoirs Illustrating the History of Jacobinism* 32, 39

BATF. *See* Bureau of Alcohol, Tobacco, and Firearms
Bavarian Court of Enquiry 32
BBC
— "Conspiracy Files" 72
Beck, Glenn 130–131
Bellamy, Edward 8
Bell, Daniel
— *Coming of Post-Industrial Society, The* 102
Beltagy, Mohamed 123
Benghazi, Libya 63–64, 133–134
Benson, Herbert 96
Bernays, Edward
— *Propaganda* 55
Best, Gary 73
Biden, Joseph 134
Billington, James
— *Fire in the Minds of Men* 30, 33, 36
Bin Laden Group 69
bin Laden, Mohammad 69
bin Laden, Osama 69, 109
Bin, Xia 128
Bin Zayed, Abdullah 113
BIS. *See* Bank for International Settlements
Bissett, James
— *Toronto Globe and Mail*—"We Have Created a Monster" 66
Blackham, H. J.
— *Humanist, The* 49
Bloomfield, Lincoln 17
Bodansky, Yossef 68
Bode, Johann 33, 36
Boehme, Jacob 38
Boehner, John 118
Bohemian Grove 30
Bojinka Project 69
Bonneville, Nicholas 36
Bonn, M. J.

[ 160 ]

— *Annals of American Academy of Political and Social Science, The* 79
Bormann, Martin 17
Bornstein, Robert
— *Journal of the Mind and Behavior*—"Subliminal Techniques as Propaganda Tools" 56
Bosnian War 66
Bourbons 21
Brand, Robert 105
Brissotine faction 50
Brownson, Orestes 15, 21, 23–24
— *Works of Orestes Brownson, The* 45
Brzezinski, Zbigniew 18, 63, 117, 127, 154
— *Between Two Ages* 154
— *Grand Chessboard, The* 112
— *Newsmax* 117
Buonarroti, Filippo Michele 36–37
Bureau of Alcohol, Tobacco, and Firearms 69, 73–74
Bureau of Social Hygiene 145
Burnes, Chevalier 11
Burrell, Paul 20
Bush, George H. W. 18, 38, 104, 107, 131, 133
Bush, George W. 19, 53, 131, 133
Bush, Jeb 20, 133–135

## C

Cabet, Etienne 44
Calhoun, Arthur
— *A Social History of the American Family* 94
Cameron, David 110
Cantor, Paul 149
Carlson, Susan
— WLS Radio 75
Carnegie, Andrew 16

Carnegie Corporation 89–90, 101
Carnegie Endowment for International Peace 99
Carnegie Forum 101
Carnegie Foundation 144
Carter, Jimmy 63, 97, 112
Castro, Fidel 65
Castro, Julian 133
Catholic Church 21, 132
CBS 63–64, 69, 88, 91
CCE. *See* Center for Civic Education
Center for Civic Education 53
— *We the People* 53
Center for Human Resource Development 96
Central Intelligence Agency 62, 66, 68, 70, 72–73, 75, 83, 105–108, 111
CFR. *See* Council on Foreign Relations
Charles, Roger 74
Chase, Stuart 90
— *A New Deal* 90
— *The Proper Study of Mankind* 89
Chesterton, G. K.
— *Everlasting Man, The* 141
Chisholm, Brock 49, 140
— *Psychiatry* 24, 48
Churchill, Winston 82
— *Saturday Evening Post, The*—"The United States of Europe" 19
CIA. *See* Central Intelligence Agency
Clauson, John 90
— *Social Psychology Quarterly*, Vol. 47—"Research on the American Soldier as a Career Contingency" 88
Clinton, Bill 19, 62, 74, 77, 96–97, 101, 103–104, 133, 152–153
Clinton, Cornelia 43

Clinton, Dewitt   43
Clinton. DeWitt   43, 52
Clinton, George   43
Clinton, Hillary   62, 64, 97–99, 117–118, 121, 133
— *It Takes A Village*   98
Coates, Dan   96
Colby, William   105
Coleman, James
— *The Adolescent Society*   149
Columbia University   24, 91, 149
Committee on Human Resources   88, 90
Compton, Bob
— "2 Million Minutes"   125
Comte, Auguste   132
— *Catechism of Positive Religion, The*   156
— *System of Positive Polity*   22, 48, 156
Copeland, Miles   108
— *Game of Nations, The*   107
Corbett, P. E.
— *Post-War Worlds*   79
Cosandey, Johann   39
Council on Foreign Relations   17–18, 77, 83, 88, 107, 111
Cousins, Norman   85
— *Modern Man Is Obsolete*   85
Cremin, Lawrence
— *Transformation of the School*   44
Crogan, Jim
— *L.A. Weekly*—"An Oklahoma Mystery: New hints of links between Timothy McVeigh and Middle Eastern terrorists"   68
Crosby, David
— *Rolling Stone*, Vol. 1   149
Crusades   10, 12

Cuban Missile Crisis   61
Cuddy, Dennis
— *Power Elite and the Secret Nazi Plan, The*   61, 68, 75, 130
Culvertson, John
— "Case Study Relating Blast Effects Tests to the Events of April 19th, 1995, Alfred P. Murrah Building, Oklahoma City, Oklahoma"   74

## D

Dalberg, Karl Theodor   35
Darkazanli, Mamoun   106
d'Arusmont, Francoise   21, 45
Darwin, Charles   22
Davis, Elmer   88
Davison, W. Phillips   88
Day, Richard   146
de Bouillon, Godfroi   10
DeCamp, John   105
Declaration of Independence   14
de Luchet, Jean Pierre Louis   34
de Molay, Jacques   10–11
de Payens, Hugues   9–10
de Ridefort, Gerard   10
de Robespierre, Maximilien   36, 50
de Sade, Marquis   46
— *La Philosophie Dans le Boudoir*   21, 46
de Saint-Simon, Henri   22, 48
de Talleyrand, Charles Maurice   51
de Tocqueville, Alexis   22
— *Democracy In America*   21
DeVinney, Leland   89
Dewey, John   24, 149
— *Humanist Manifesto*   23, 38, 48
D'Eyncourt, Chevalier (Charles) Tennyson   11
Dickopf, Paul   145

Directorate for Inter-Services Intelligence   72
Dodd, Norman   17, 84
Dodson, Dan   137
Dole, Bob   99, 103
Dollard, Charles   89–90
Donovan, Jennifer
— *San Francisco Chronicle*—"Creating Mythos of the Modern World"   98
Dougherty, Jon
— WorldNetDaily—"Iraq link to OKC, Sept. 11 attacks?"   70
Douglas, William O.   86
— *Towards a Global Federalism*   85
Dreyfuss, Robert
— *Devil's Game: How the United States Helped Unleash Fundamentalist Islam*   108
Drucker, Peter   153
Dulles, Allen   61, 68, 75, 108
Dulles, Eleanor   61
Dulles, John Foster   61–62, 80
— "Toward World Order"   80
Dulman, Richard
— *Der Geheimbund Der Illuminatum*   37
Durant, Will and Ariel
— *Rousseau and Revolution*   28
Dwight, Timothy   40

E

Eagleton, Clyde   80
— *International Government*   78
Earth Charter   100, 128, 155
*Economist, The*—January 9, 1988   128–129
Ecozoic Era   154–155
ECS. *See* Education Commission of the States
Education Commission of the States   92
Egyptian Islamic Jihad   73
"Egypt's Muslim Brotherhood"   111
Eisenhower, Dwight D.   68, 80, 108
Eisenstein, Elizabeth
— *First Professional Revolutionist: Filippo Michele Buonarroti (1761-1837), The*   36
El-Balad   122
El-Baradei, Mohamed   124
El-Deeb, Sarah
— Associated Press   114
Elizabeth, Queen of England   20
Ellison, Keith   120
El Morya   95–96
Elohim City, Oklahoma   69, 73
Emerson, Steven
— *American Jihad: The Terrorists Living Among Us*   68
Emery, Fred   151
— *Futures We Are In*   87
*Encyclopedia of Mythology, The*   99
*Encyclopedia of Occultism & Parapsychology*   98
Engels, Friedrich   37, 44
*Engel v. Vital*   24
Engineers Syndicate   110
Ernst, Ludwig II   33
Esher, Lord   16
Estikhabarat   71
EU. *See* European Union
European Union   19, 82, 86, 127, 131
Evans-Pritchard, Ambrose   74–75
— *Secret Life of Bill Clinton: The Unreported Stories, The*   74

F

Fabian Socialism   9, 31

Fannie Mae   64
FBI. *See* Federal Bureau of Investigation
FDR. *See* Roosevelt, Franklin
Federal Bureau of Investigation   69, 73–74
Federal Council of Churches
— *A Basis for the Peace to Come*   80, 84
— "Commission to Study the Basis of a Just and Durable Peace"   79
Federal Reserve Act   16
Ferdinand, Franz   65
Fichte, Johann Gottlieb   34
Finley, Angela   73–74
Fisk, Robert
— *Independent, The*—"The demise of the dollar"   128
FJP. *See* Freedom and Justice Party
Fletcher, Bob   73
Forbes, Steve   86
Ford Foundation   17, 84, 88–89, 103, 149
Fosdick, Raymond   87, 145
Foster, William Z.
— *Toward Soviet America*   46
Foundation for Excellence in Education   134
Frankfurt School   149
— Institute for Social Research   149
Franklin, Benjamin   14
Freddie Mac   64
Frederick Augustus I   34
Frederick William II, King of Prussia   34
Freedom and Justice Party   113–115
Free Egyptians Party   114
Free World
— *Round Table No. 10*—"Coming World Order, The"   80
— *Round Table No. 11*—"Prospects for 1942"   81
French Revolution   21–22, 33, 35–36, 40, 46, 50–51, 132
Freneau, Philip   14, 65, 136–137
— American Museum—"Rules for Changing a Limited Republican Government into an Unlimited Hereditary One"   14, 65, 136

**G**

Gaither, H. Rowan   17, 84
Gandhi, Mahatma   98
Gardner, John   90
Gates, Frederick   47
— *Occasional Letter, No. 1*   47
GATT. *See* General Agreement on Tariffs and Trade
Gehlen Organization   75
Gehlen, Reinhard   75
General Agreement on Tariffs and Trade   64, 81, 100, 102–103, 105
General Motors   64
Genet, Edmond Charles (Citizen)   39, 41, 43, 50–51
George III, King of England   14
Georgetown University   77
George Washington University   121
German Union   35
Glaser, Edward   149
— *An Experiment in the Development of Critical Thinking*   149
Glaspie, April   66
Glick, Caroline
— *Jerusalem Post, The*   111
— *Jewish World Review*   115
*Global Muslim Brotherhood Daily Report*   112

Goebbels, Joseph   23
Goethe, Johann   36
Golitsyn, Anatoliy
— *Perestroika Deception, The*   86
Gorbachev, Mikhail   18, 79, 86, 148, 155
— International Green Cross   155
Gorbachev, Raisa   86
Gore, Al   96, 98
— *Earth in the Balance*   98
Gramsci, Antonio   86, 148
Grand Orient Lodge of Des Amis Sincères   36
Grand Orient Masonic Lodge of France   33
Green Shirts. *See* Young Egypt
Gregg, Alan   87
Grey, Edward   65
Gross, Bertram
— *Friendly Fascism: The New Face of Power in America*   150–151
Grunberger, Georg   39

# H

Hagger, Nicholas
— *Syndicate: The Story of the Coming World Government, The*   20
Hall, G. Stanley   38
Hamas   68, 106, 108
Hamida, Ragib Hilal   111
Hand, Brevard   25
Hannity, Sean   130–131
Harley, John Eugene
— *International Understanding: Agencies Educating for a New World*   78
Harman, Willis   59

Harvard Capital Group   76
Harvard Medical School   96
Harvard University   89
Hayden, Mike   69, 111
Hegazy, Safwat   122
Hegel, George   34–35
Hertel, Jakob   30
Himmler, Heinrich   17
Hiss, Alger   24
Hitler, Adolph   63, 68, 106–107
— *Mein Kampf*   107
Hitler Youth   72
Hoechst AG   145
*Holy Bible, The*   21, 24, 157
Homeland Security Act   60, 152
Horkheimer, Max   149
Horowitz, David   120
Hosenball, Mark
— *Newsweek*   106
Hospitallers   12
Houghton, Raymond   138
House, Edward M.   16, 62
— *Philip Dru: Administrator*   16
House Homeland Security Committee   64
Houston, Jean   97–100
— "Myth and Mystery of Isis and Osiris: A Journey of Transformation, The"   99
— *Passion of Isis and Osiris: A Union of Two Souls, The*   99
— "Rise of the New Right, The"   97
— "Whole System Transition: The Birth of the Planetary Society"   97
Howard, Graeme
— *America and a New World Order*   79
Howe, Carol   73–74

Hull, Cordell   99
Hull, Thomas   25
*Humanist Manifesto*   25, 38
*Human Relations*   87
Hunt, James B. Jr.   47
Husain, Ed   111
Hussein, Ahmed   107
Hussein, Saddam   66, 70–71, 109
Huxley, Aldous
— *Brave New World Revisited*   19
Huxley, Julian   144

## I

I.G. Farben   146
Ignatius, David
— *Lebanon Daily Star*   115
Illuminati   7, 21, 28–44, 46–47, 49, 51–53
Illuminati Online   53
"Illuminati Provincial Report"   37
Illuminatus Minor   31, 38
Imprisoned Omar Abdul Rahman Brigades   63
Intercollegiate Socialist Society, The   89
International Humanist and Ethical Union   49
International Labor Organization   99
International Socialist Organization   151
Interpol   145
Iraqi Military Intelligence Service   71
Iraq War   66
Iridium   69
ISI. *See* Directorate for Inter-Services Intelligence
Isikoff, Michael
— *Newsweek*   106
Islamic Jihad   73, 106, 109
Ismail, Farrag
— *Al-Gumbouriya*   117
Israel News Update   111
Issues in Training   87
Italian Carbonari   37

## J

Jackson, Andrew   15, 17
Jackson, C. D.   88
Jackson, Steve
— "Illuminati: New World Order: Assassins"   53
Jacobin Club   52
James II, King of England   14
James IV, King of Scotland   12
Jarrett, Valerie   62
"Jazira Plan"   121
Jefferson, Thomas   41–43, 50–51
*Jerusalem Post, The*   110–111
Jesuits. *See* Society of Jesus
Jibril, Mahmoud   115
John Doe 2   71
Johnson, Lyndon B.   38, 90
Johnston, John M.   70

## K

Karier, Clarence
— *Individual, Society, and Education: A History of American Educational Ideas, The*   47
Karzai, Hamid   62
Kassebaum, Nancy   96
Khalfan, Dahi   112–113, 124
Khalil, Lydia   111
Khayyam, Omar   9
Khomeini, Ruholla   63, 117
King, Peter   63–64
King Saud of Saudi Arabia   107
KLA. *See* Kosovo Liberation Army

Klein, G. S.
— *Journal of Abnormal and Social Psychology*–"Subliminal Effects of Verbal Stimuli"   57
Knights Templar   7, 9–12, 33
Knights Templars, The   12
*Knight Templar* (1987)   12
Knoke, William   76, 105
— *Bold New World: The Essential Road Map to the Twenty-First Century*   76, 83, 86, 104
Kohl, Helmut   72
Korean War   18, 65
Korten, David C.
— *When Corporations Rule the World*   103–104
Koselleck, Reinhart
— *Critique and Crisis: Enlightenment and the Modern Society*   34, 48
Kosovo Liberation Army   66

**L**

Langan, Peter   73
Lang, Patrick   71
Langston, James
— *Evening Standard*—"Iraqis Linked to Oklahoma Atrocity"   70–71
Larmenius, John Mark   10
Lasswell, Harold   88, 90
Lawrence, Richard   15
Lawson, Thomas
— *Frenzied Finance*   16
Lazard Brothers   105
League for Industrial Democracy   89
League of Nations   16, 77, 99
League of Nations Institute for Intellectual Cooperation   77
League of the Just   15, 36–37

Lee, Martin
— *Razor Magazine*   109–110
LeForestier, Rene   33
— *Les Illumines de Baviere et la Franc-Maconnerie Allemande*   33–34
Lenin, Vladimir   85–86
— *Collected Works*   19
Les Amis Reunis Lodge   33
Lewin, Kurt   87, 92, 151
Lewis, Michael   26
Libet, Benjamin
— *Brain and Behavioral Sciences, The*   59
Lichnowsky, Karl Max   65
Lilienthal, Alfred
— *Which Way to World Government?*   81
Limbaugh, Rush   130–131
Lincoln, Abraham   25
Lippmann, Walter   88
"Locksley Hall"   11, 15, 173
Lodge of the Nine Sisters   39
Loftus, John; Aarons, Mark
— *Secret War Against the Jews, The*   68
*Los Angeles Times*—"Lenin Aims Like U.N.'s, Thant Says"   85
Loughary, John   138
Lucifer   27, 38, 49, 135
Lucifer Publishing Co.   38, 96, 157
Lucis Trust   96
Luckert, Steven
— *Jesuits, Freemasons, Illuminati, and Jacobins: Conspiracy theories, secret societies, and politics in late eighteenth-century Germany*   32
Lukacs, Gyorgy   148
Luria, Alexander   151
Lyons, Kirk   72–74

## M

Mackey, Albert
— *Lexicon of Freemasonry*   10
Madison, James   41
Maidment, J.   12
Mann, Horace   44
Mantoux, Paul
— *International Understanding: Agencies Educating for a New World*   78
Marcuse, Herbert   149
Marshall, George   17, 65
Marshall, John   88
Marx, Karl   7, 15–16, 22–23, 37, 48, 130
— *Communist Manifesto*   7, 15, 22, 37, 44
Masonic Peace Conference   19
Masters, Robert   99
Mauldin, W. Parker   89
Mauro, Ryan
— radicalislam.org   121–122
Mazzini, Giuseppe   37
MB. *See* Muslim Brotherhood
McCain, John   118
McCloy, John Jay   14, 88
McConnell, James
— *Esquire*   138
McCune, Shirley   92–97, 99, 101
— Arizona State University   95
— "Framing a Future for Education"   92
— *Light Shall Set You Free, The*   95
McKittrick, Thomas   17
McPeak, William   89
McREL. *See* Mid-Continent Regional Educational Laboratory
McVeigh, Timothy   68–73, 75
Melanson, Terry
— *Illuminati Conspiracy Archive*   29, 34, 36, 44
Merkel, Angela   19
Meyer, Cord Jr.   83
— *New York Herald Tribune Forum*   83
— *Peace or Anarchy?*   82
Michigan State University   145
Mid-Continent Regional Educational Laboratory   92
Millar, Robert   73
Milner, Alfred   106
Milner Group   106
Milosevic, Slobodan   66
Minerval Assembly   30
Minerval Degree   30
Minervals   34
Mingo Creek Democratic Society   39
Minor, Robert   16
Mirabeau, Honore   33, 51
Mohamed, Ali   73
Mohammed, Khalid Sheikh   109
Monroe, Will
— *History of the Pestalozzian Movement in the United States*   43
Morgan, J. P.   7, 16, 41
Morin, William
— *Baltimore Sun*   104
— *Successful Termination*   104
Morris, Adam   105
Morrison, Mitch
— *Wall Street Journal, The*—"Iraq Connection, The"   71
Morse, Chuck
— *Nazi Connection to Islamic Terrorism, The*   71
Morse, Jedediah   39, 42
Morsi, Mohamed   62–64, 115–116, 118–124

Mossadegh, Mohammad   63
Motley, John Lothrop   15
Moussaoui, Zacarias   70
Mubarak, Hosni   110, 114, 116–117, 119–121, 123
Muller, Robert   96
— "Educating the Global Citizen: Illuminating the Issues"   97
Murad, Abdul Hakim   69–70
Muslim Brotherhood   8, 17, 20, 62, 64, 68–70, 106–124, 130
Muslim Sisterhood   118, 121
Muslim Students Association   121

## N

Nada, Youssef   106
NAFTA. See North American Free Trade Agreement
Naisbitt Group   92
Naisbitt, John   97–98
— *Megatrends*   92
Nasser, Gamal Abdel   62, 107–109
National Catholic Educational Association   97
National Center on Education and the Economy   101
"National Commission on Human Resource Development Act"   96
National Defense Council   119
National Education Association   87, 97, 137
National Security Agency   69, 154
National Socialism   16–17, 23, 130
National Training Laboratories   87, 92, 99
*National Treasure*   9
NATO   66
Nazis   16–18, 23, 61–62, 68, 72, 75, 107, 130, 141, 148
NCEE. See National Center on Education and the Economy
NEA. See National Education Association
Neilson, William Allan   80
New Harmony, Indiana   15, 21, 45
New Jersey Robert Wood Johnson Medical School   26
*Newsweek*   96
— "Megatrends Man, The"   98
Newtown, Connecticut   60
*New York Post*   63
*New York Times, The*   97, 111
Nichols, Terry   69–71, 73
Nixon, Richard   131, 133
— *Foreign Affairs*   18
*Noble Lie, A*   74
No Child Left Behind Act of 2001   53
North American Free Trade Agreement   19, 64, 103, 127
Notre Dame Cathedral   21
NSA. See National Security Agency
NTL. See National Training Laboratories

## O

Obama, Barack   8, 19–20, 53, 62–64, 85–86, 100, 112, 115, 117–118, 127–128, 130–135, 144
OBE. See outcome-based education
Office of Strategic Services   72, 75
Office of War Information   88, 90–91
Oklahoma City bombing   7, 68–75
O'Meara, Kelly Patricia
— *Insight Magazine*—"Iraq Connections to U.S. Extremists"   71
Order of Sion   10
"Order of the Knights of St. John and the Temple."   12

Order of the Temple (of Solomon)   9
*Orlando Sentinel*—"Beware subliminal messages in media"   57
OSS. *See* Office of Strategic Services
outcome-based education   101
Owen, Robert   21, 44–45
Owen, Robert Dale   15, 21, 23, 45
OWI. *See* Office of War Information
Oxford University   16, 22, 37–38, 88

**P**

Paige, Rod   19
Paley, William   88
Palmer, Elizabeth   63–64
Panetta, Leon   119
Parish, Elijah
— "An Oration Delivered at Byfield"   49
Patriot Act   60, 152
Patterson, James; Kim, Peter
— *Day America Told the Truth— What People Really Believe About Everything That Really Matters, The*   26
Payson, Seth
— *Proofs of the Real Existence, and Dangerous Tendency, of Illuminism*   50
Pearl Harbor   65, 107
Pell, Claiborne   96
Pentagon   53, 66, 69, 71, 152
*Perfektibilisten*   28
Permanent Normal Trade Relations with Communist China   64
Perry, Tom
— *Reuters*—"Brotherhood man promises Islamic law in Egypt"   121
Pestalozzi, Johann Heinrich   35, 43–44, 47
Petruskie, Vincent   72
Philadelphes   33
Philip IV, King of France   10–11
Phoenix   128, 132, 147
Pike, Albert   11, 38
— *Morals and Dogma*   38
Pinkard, Terry
— *Hegel: A Biography*   34
Planetary Citizens   85
Planned Parenthood   23, 46, 146
Plato
— *Republic*   22
Pope, Alexander   12
population control   21, 32, 47
Population Council   89, 146
Porset, Charles   33
Porter, Elsa   97
Positivist philosophy   22
Possible Society, The   97
Potter, Charles Francis
— *Humanism: A New Religion*   23, 48
— *Humanist Manifesto*   23
Princess Mary of England   14
Project Bojinka   69
Putnam School—Minneapolis, MN   155

**Q**

Qasim, Abd al-Karim   70
Quigley, Carroll
— *Tragedy and Hope*   77
Qutb, Sayyid   109

**R**

Radio Liberty   73, 130
Rahman, Omar Abdul   63, 115, 121
RAND   88, 90
Rattner, Justin   157
Raymond, Bernard   11
Reagan, Ronald   18, 131, 134

Reece Committee   17
Rees, John R.   24, 151–152
— *Mental Health*   23
Reich, Robert
— *Work of Nations, The*   101
Research Center for Group Dynamics   87, 92
Reuters   112
Rhodes, Cecil   16, 19, 22, 37–38, 41, 77, 79–80, 105–106
Rice, Susan   64
Richard the Lion-Hearted   10–11
Rickel, Peter   73
Robert Muller School   96
Robison, John
— *Proofs of a Conspiracy*   28–31, 35, 38–39, 42
Rockefeller, David   18, 127
— *Memoirs*   20, 127
Rockefeller Foundation   87–89, 144
Rockefeller General Education Board   47, 87, 145
Rockefeller, John D.   7, 16, 130
Rockefeller, John D. III   146
Rockefeller, John D. Jr.   145
Rockefeller, Nelson   18, 61
*Roe v. Wade*   25
Rohatyn, Felix   105
Rohricht, R.
— *Regesta Regni Hierosolymitani*   10
Rokeach, Milton
— *Psychology Today*—"Persuasion That Persists"   55, 138
Romney, Mitt   64, 131, 133
Roosevelt, Clinton
— *Science of Government Founded in Natural Law, The*   52
Roosevelt, Eleanor   98
Roosevelt, Franklin   16, 52, 64–65, 90, 100, 107

Rosenbaum, Ron
— *Esquire*—"Last Secrets of Skull and Bones"   52
Round Table Groups   77, 80, 105
Rousseau, Jean Jacques   33, 36
— *Social Contract*   36
Roussel-Uclaf   145
Royal Institute of International Affairs   77
RU-486   146
Rubio, Marco   133
Rusk, Dean   17
Ruskin, John   15–16, 22, 37
Russell, Bertrand   144
— *Impact of Science on Society, The*   55
Russell, William H.   47

## S

Sabahi, Hamdeen   124
Sabbah, Hasan-i   9
Sadat, Anwar   107, 109–110
Sage, Russell   89
Said, Ahmed   114
Saint-Martin   38
Saladin   12
Salah, Kahlid   122
Salah, Raed   112
Saleh, Sobhi
— *Al-Masry Al-Youm*   111
Sale, Richard
— "Exclusive: Saddam key in early CIA plot"   70
Salwa movement   113
Samuel, Herbert   106
Sanger, Margaret   22, 46
— *Birth Control Review*   23
— *Pivot of Civilization*   23
Sargant, William
— *Battle for the Mind: The Mechanics of Indoctrination,*

*Brainwashing, and Thought Control* 57
Sassoli, Alessandro
— *Coin Update*—September 1, 2010 128
Savioli, Ludvig 30
S&B. *See* Skull & Bones
Schlosser, Friedrich Christoph
— *History of the eighteenth century and of the nineteenth till the overthrow of the French Empire: With particular reference to mental cultivation and progress* 29
school-to-work 89, 101, 148
Schuttler, Hermann
— *Die Mitglieder des Illuminatenordens 1776-1787/93* 35
Science Research Associates 89
Scroll & Key 82
Second Bank of the United States 15
Secret Society of the Elect 16, 22, 37, 41
September 11, 2001 60, 66, 152
Sewell, Thomas 15
Shafiq, Ahmed 116, 120
sharia law 63, 111, 114, 120–122
Shaw, George Bernard 146
Shelley, Percy Bysshe 36
"Shiite Crescent" 122
Shotwell, James T. 99–100
— *Autobiography of James T. Shotwell, The* 99
Simpson, Christopher
— *Science of Coercion: Communication Research and Psychological Warfare 1945–1960* 56, 88, 90, 91
Sizer, Ted 26

— *Five Lectures … On Moral Education* 24, 49
Skull & Bones 16, 35, 47, 52, 107, 133
Smith, G. J. W
— *Journal of Abnormal and Social Psychology*–"Subliminal Effects of Verbal Stimuli" 57
Smithsonian Institute 46
Smith, William Sidney 10–11
Snyder, David
— *Futurist, The*—"Revolution in the Workplace: What's Happening to Our Jobs?, The" 101
Snyder, G. W. 39
*Socialist Worker*—November 22, 1996 151
Social Science Research Council 89
Society for Psychical Research 11
Society of Jesus 28, 32
Soong, T. V.
— *Free World*—"Coming International Order, The" 81
Soros, George 131
Southwestern Oklahoma State University 69
Soviet-American Exchange Agreement 18, 101
Spanish-American War 65
Spence, D. P.
— *Journal of Abnormal and Social Psychology*–"Subliminal Effects of Verbal Stimuli" 57
Spencer, Lyle 89
Springborg, Robert 119
Stalin, Joseph 19, 107
Stamp Act 14
Stanford University 59
State of the World Forum 18, 79, 127

Steinem, Gloria   140
Sterne, Laurence
— *Life and Opinions of Tristram Shandy, Gentleman, The*   47
Stettinius, Edward   107
Stimson, Henry   107
Stofft, William
— *World 2010: A Decline of Superpower Influence, A*   102
Stolberg, Sheryl
— *New York Times*—July 20, 1998   153
Stouffer, Samuel   88, 90
— Harvard University   88
Strassmeir, Andreas   69, 72–75
Strassmeir, Gunter   72
Strobl, Johann
— *Original Writing of the Illuminati*   32
— *Supplement of Further Original Works*   32
STW. *See* school-to-work
*Sublimes Maîtres Parfaits*   36
"Suckernomics"   127
Supreme Council of the Armed Forces, The   119
Sutton, Antony
— *America's Secret Establishment: An Introduction to the Order of Skull & Bones*   35
Swedenborg, Emanuel   38
Sweidan, Tareq
— Al-Quds TV   112
Swift, Jonathan   12
Swing, William
— "United Religions"   79

## T

Taliban   66
Talmon, J. L.
— *Rise of Totalitarian Democracy, The*   36
Tantawi, Hussein   118–120
Tappan, David
— "Discourse Delivered in the Chapel of Harvard College, June 19, 1798, A"   51
Tavistock Institute for Medical Psychology   23
Tavistock Institute of Human Relations   87
Taylor, Charles W.
— *World 2010: A New Order of Nations, A*   102
Technozoic Era   154
*Telegraph, The* [London]—"America's Secret Backing for Rebel Leaders Behind Uprising"   110
Temple of Understanding   97
Temple, William   12, 14
Tennyson, Alfred Lord   11, 15–17
— "Locksley Hall"   11, 15
Thant, U   84, 85
— Uppsala University   84
Theistical Society   42
*Time* magazine   63, 91, 119, 123
Toynbee, Arnold   76, 77
— *Fourth Annual Conference of Institutions for the Scientific Study of International Relations*   77
— *International Affairs*   77
Trilateral Commission   18, 127
*Trumpet*   52
Tulfah, Khairullah   71

## U

UFWC. *See* United Future World Currency
U.N.. *See* United Nations
UNESCO   19, 85, 90, 96–97, 144–145

— *UNESCO: Its Purpose and Its Philosophy*  145
UNESCO Associated Schools Project  96
Union of Socialist Democratic Republics  100
United Future World Currency  128–129
United Nations  17, 62, 82–85, 96, 99, 105, 153, 155–156
United Nations Fourth World Conference on Women  153
United States of Europe  19
United World Federalists  82
University at Ingolstadt  28
University of California, San Francisco  59
University of Leipzig  37
University of Michigan  55, 138
University of Michigan—Research Center for Group Dynamics  87
U.S. Conference of Mayors  128, 155
U.S. Department of Education  149
USDR. *See* Union of Socialist Democratic Republics
U.S. Justice Department  152
*U.S. News & World Report*— "Washington Whispers"  71
*U.S.S. Maine*  65
U.S.S.R.  18
Utzschneider, Joseph  39

**V**

van Dulman, Richard
— *Der Geheimbund Der Illuminatum*  37
Veon, Joan  103
Vietnam War  17, 66, 137
von Bolschwing, Otto  68
von Gochhausen, Ernst
— *Exposure of the Cosmopolitan System: In Letters from ex-Freemasons*  31, 53
von Knigge, Adolph  31–32, 49

**W**

Wallace, William Kay  78
— *Our Obsolete Constitution*  78
Warren, Rick  153
Washington, George  39, 41, 51
Weishaupt, Adam  21, 27–30, 32–33, 35, 37–38, 41–42, 44, 46, 48–52
Wells, H. G.  90, 133
— *New World Order, The*  133
— *New Worlds for Old*  31
— *Shape of Things to Come, The*  17
Welt Online—"Europe's foreign ministers want more power for EU"  19
Wharton, Thomas  14
Whiskey Rebellion  39, 41
Whitney, William  35, 133
Willard, Joseph  43
William of Orange  14
Williams, Paul
— *Al-Qaeda: Brotherhood of Terror*  69
Willis, Ellen
— *Nation, The*  25
Willkie, Wendell  64
Wilson, Woodrow  16, 62, 78
*Wonderful Wizard of Oz, The*  97
Wood, John
— *Full Exposition of the Clintonian Faction and the Society of the Columbian Illuminati, A*  42
Woodward, Bob  99

— *Choice, The* 97
— *Washington Post, The* 97–98
Workingmen's Party 15, 21, 45
World Association of World Federalists 84
World Bank 88, 153
World Federalist Association 85
World Federation of Nations 20, 27, 129, 135, 157
World Health Organization 24, 48, 140
World Movement for World Federal Government 81
world socialist government 7–8, 17–18, 20, 27, 86, 100, 102, 105, 129–131, 133, 135, 146
World Trade Center 53, 63, 66, 69, 115, 121, 152
World Trade Organization 81, 100, 103–104, 147
World War I 65–66, 78
World War II 17, 62, 65–66, 72, 75, 80, 83, 88, 106–107
Wright, Fanny 21, 23
Wright, Frances 15, 45
Wright, George 11–12
WTO. *See* World Trade Organization
Wundt, Kirchenrat Karl Kasimir 37
Wundt, Wilhelm 37–38

## Y

Yale University 16, 40, 47, 52, 62, 82, 107
*Youm-7* 122
Younes, Ali
— *Al-Arabiya News*—"Military council and constitutional court pose threat to democracy in Egypt" 116
Young, Donald 89
Young Egypt 107

Youssef, Ramzi 69–70

## Z

Zwack, Franz 30

 Dennis Laurence Cuddy, historian and political analyst, received a Ph.D. from the University of North Carolina at Chapel Hill (major in American history, minor in political science). Dr. Cuddy has taught at the university level, has been a political and economic risk analyst for an international consulting firm, and has been a senior associate with the U.S. Department of Education.

Cuddy has also testified before members of Congress on behalf of the U.S. Department of Justice. Dr. Cuddy has authored or edited twenty-five books and booklets, and has written hundreds of articles appearing in newspapers around the nation, including *The Washington Post, Los Angeles Times* and *USA Today*. He has been a guest on numerous radio talk shows in various parts of the country, such as ABC Radio in New York City, and he has also been a guest on the national television programs "USA Today" and CBS's "Nightwatch."